ROUTLEDGE LIBRARY EDITIONS: INTERNATIONAL SECURITY STUDIES

Volume 2

CODEBREAKING AND SIGNALS INTELLIGENCE

CODEBREAKING AND SIGNALS INTELLIGENCE

Edited by
CHRISTOPHER ANDREW

LONDON AND NEW YORK

First published in 1986 by Frank Cass and Company Limited

This edition first published in 2021
by Routledge
2 Park Square, Milton Park, Abingdon, Oxon OX14 4RN

and by Routledge
52 Vanderbilt Avenue, New York, NY 10017

Routledge is an imprint of the Taylor & Francis Group, an informa business

© 1986 Frank Cass & Co. Ltd

All rights reserved. No part of this book may be reprinted or reproduced or utilised in any form or by any electronic, mechanical, or other means, now known or hereafter invented, including photocopying and recording, or in any information storage or retrieval system, without permission in writing from the publishers.

Trademark notice: Product or corporate names may be trademarks or registered trademarks, and are used only for identification and explanation without intent to infringe.

British Library Cataloguing in Publication Data
A catalogue record for this book is available from the British Library

ISBN: 978-0-367-68499-0 (Set)
ISBN: 978-1-00-316169-1 (Set) (ebk)
ISBN: 978-0-367-70875-7 (Volume 2) (hbk)
ISBN: 978-0-367-70879-5 (Volume 2) (pbk)
ISBN: 978-1-00-314832-6 (Volume 2) (ebk)

Publisher's Note
The publisher has gone to great lengths to ensure the quality of this reprint but points out that some imperfections in the original copies may be apparent.

Disclaimer
The publisher has made every effort to trace copyright holders and would welcome correspondence from those they have been unable to trace.

CODEBREAKING
AND
SIGNALS
INTELLIGENCE

Edited by
Christopher Andrew

FRANK CASS

First published 1986 in Great Britain by
FRANK CASS AND COMPANY LIMITED
Gainsborough House, 11 Gainsborough Road,
London E11 1RS, England

and in the United States of America by
FRANK CASS AND COMPANY LIMITED
c/o Biblio Distribution Center,
81 Adams Drive, P.O. Box 327, Totawa, NJ 07511

Copyright © 1986 Frank Cass & Co. Ltd

Codebreaking and signals intelligence.—
 (Intelligence and national security; 1)
 1. Cryptography—History
 I. Andrew, Christopher H.   II. Series
 355.3'432   UB290

ISBN 0–7146–3299–6

This group of studies first appeared in a Special Issue on 'Code-breaking and National Security' of the journal *Intelligence and National Security*, Vol. 1, No. 1, published by Frank Cass and Co. Ltd.

All rights reserved. No part of this publication may be reproduced, stored in a retrieval system or transmitted in any form or by any means, electronic, mechanical, photocopying, recording or otherwise, without prior permission of Frank Cass and Company Limited.

Printed in Great Britain by
Specialised Printing Services Ltd, Loughton, Essex

Contents

Notes on Contributors		v
Codebreaking and Signals Intelligence	*Christopher Andrew*	1
Tsarist Codebreakers and British Codes	*Christopher Andrew and Keith Neilson*	6
No Final Solution: A Survey of the Cryptanalytical Capabilities of German Military Agencies, 1926–35	*J. W. M. Chapman*	13
The Government Code and Cypher School Between the Wars	*A. G. Denniston*	48
From Polish Bomba to British Bombe: The Birth of Ultra	*Gordon Welchman*	71
Ultra's Poor Relations	*Chistopher Morris*	111
Surveillance and Intelligence under the Vichy Regime: The Service du Contrôle Technique, 1939–45	*Roger Austin*	123

Notes on Contributors

Dr Christopher Andrew is Fellow and Senior Tutor of Corpus Christi College, Cambridge. His most recent books are *The Missing Dimension: Governments and Intelligence Communities in the Twentieth Century*, in collaboration with David Dilks (London: Macmillan; Champaign, Illinois: University of Illinois Press, 1984) and *Secret Service: The Making of the British Intelligence Community* (London: Heinemann, 1985; for publication in New York by Viking early in 1986). He has written and broadcast on a variety of other historical subjects ranging from the French overseas empire to association football.

Dr Roger Austin is Lecturer in Education (History) at the University of Ulster at Coleraine. He is co-editor (with Roderick Kedward) of *Vichy France and the Resistance: Culture and Ideology* (London: Croom Helm, 1985) and the author of several articles on modern French history.

Dr John W. M. Chapman is Lecturer in International Relations at the University of Sussex. His research interests include both Asian and European contemporary history. He is the author of *The Price of Admiralty: The War Diary of the German Naval Attaché in Japan, 1939–1943* (Ripe, Sussex: Saltire Press; Vol. I: 1982; Vol. II: 1984).

The late **A. G. 'Alastair' Denniston** CBE, CMG (1881–1961) taught modern languages at Osborne Naval College and also played hockey for Scotland before the First World War. In 1914 he became one of the first recruits to Room 40 OB, the cryptanalytical unit in the Admiralty. From 1919 to 1942 he was head of the Government Code and Cypher School. After leaving Bletchley Park in 1942, he headed a civil cryptanalytical unit in London until his retirement in 1945.

Christopher Morris is now retired after many years teaching history at King's College, Cambridge, of which he is a Fellow. During the Second World War he worked at Bletchley Park on German naval ciphers. His publications cover a wide historical span from Plato to Montesquieu and from Shakespeare's politics to bubonic plague. His most recent book is a new edition of *The Illustrated Journeys of Celia Fiennes* (London: Macdonald, 1982).

Dr Keith Neilson is Assistant Professor in the Department of History at the Royal Military College of Canada, Kingston, Ontario. He is the author of *Strategy and Supply: The Anglo-Russian Alliance* (London: Allen & Unwin, 1984) and of a number of articles on modern British and Russian history.

Gordon Welchman was lecturer in Mathematics at Cambridge University and Fellow of Sidney Sussex College before the Second World War. During the War he played a key role in the work of Bletchley Park which he describes in his book *The Hut Six Story*: *Breaking the Enigma Codes* (London: Allen Lane; New York: McGraw-Hill, 1982). He is now a US citizen.

Codebreaking and Signals Intelligence

CHRISTOPHER ANDREW

This collection of essays is mainly devoted to the most important form of twentieth-century intelligence gathering before the emergence of the spy satellite: signals intelligence (sigint) derived from various technologies of interception and the work of codebreakers and cryptanalysts. The final article, however, is a reminder of the continued importance of much more traditional forms of message interception. The ancient, if often dubious, art of the letter-opener still survives in an intelligence era increasingly dominated by ever more sophisticated means of technical collection.

Despite the massive publicity over the last decade given to the successes of British and American codebreakers against the Germans and Japanese during the Second World War, the study of sigint – particularly in peacetime – is still in its infancy. Governments have usually sought to preserve the fiction that, except in time of war, they follow the maxim of Henry Stimson, American Secretary of State from 1929 to 1933, that 'Gentlemen do not read each other's mail'. Not until 1983, when Geoffrey Prime was found guilty of passing British sigint secrets to the Russians, did the British government finally acknowledge that the sigint agency based at Cheltenham, the Government Communications Head-Quarters (GCHQ), has 'an intelligence role'. The government continues to insist that, although much sigint for the two world wars is now available in the Public Record Office, even the most elderly peacetime sigint must remain secret indefinitely.

The reasons for Whitehall's remarkable historical reticence (which, in the nicest possible way, this volume seeks to sabotage) are set out in a secret memorandum of 8 September 1920 sent by the cabinet secretary, Maurice Hankey, to the prime minister, David Lloyd George. 'If it becomes known that we decoded ... messages,' he warns in giving the first of his reasons, 'all the Governments of the world will probably soon discover that no messages are safe. To a certain extent, however, this is already known.' The second reason for preserving total secrecy about sigint is, according to Hankey, 'that public opinion may experience a shock if it realises what has been going on'. Though the first of these arguments in particular continues to impress Whitehall, neither provides any credible reason for continued censorship of the historical record. If Third World governments have still not grasped that the great powers spend much of their intelligence budget on sigint, the release of interwar intercepts is unlikely to do much to disabuse them. And, despite recent revelations about GCHQ, the British public shows no sign of the state of shock that Hankey predicted.

The most successful *cabinets noirs* (as cryptanalytical agencies were then known) before the First World War were those in France and Russia. Sigint is central to an understanding of French policy to Germany during, for example, the First Moroccan Crisis of 1905 and the Agadir crisis of 1911.[2] Much less is known about the influence of sigint on Tsarist foreign policy. It is not discussed at all in two valuable recent studies of Russian policy on the eve of the First World War.[3] There is no doubt, however, that decrypted diplomatic telegrams had an important influence on Russian, as well as French, policy to the Kaiser's Germany. In 1901, for example, Count V.N. Lamsdorff, the Russian foreign minister, concluded after studying German intercepts that despite 'friendly verbal outpourings' Germany was seeking 'to hamper the realization of Russia's tasks within the Ottoman Empire'.[4] The *cabinet noir* at the Russian foreign ministry, vigorously directed from 1901 to 1910 by Aleksandr Savinsky, may actually have been more influential than its French counterpart with which it co-operated from time to time.[5]

The article by Keith Neilson and myself seeks to cast new light on the way in which the Tsarist *cabinet noir* penetrated British code and cipher systems. It also reveals a curious historical irony. Some of the Tsarist expertise used to break British codes later assisted the British to break Soviet codes after the Bolshevik Revolution.

John Chapman's study of German military codebreaking from 1926 to 1935 represents a major advance in our understanding of cryptanalysis during the Weimar Republic. The rivalry which he describes between military and naval codebreakers in Weimar Germany is reminiscent of that in Britain during the First World War and in the United States between the wars.[6] No historian of Weimar foreign or defence policy can henceforth afford to ignore the influence of sigint. But the task of relating the thousands of decrypts provided by German cryptanalysts to the policy-making process remains a formidable one, complicated both by large gaps in the archives and by interdepartmental rivalry between the foreign and defence ministries. The main target of military cryptanalysts was Poland, and the defence ministry commonly used secret intelligence to support its claims of a Polish threat to Danzig and East Prussia. The foreign ministry took a less alarmist view. Sadly, because of the destruction of the records of the *Forschungsamt*, the main cryptanalytical agency of the Nazi era, we are never likely to find evidence on sigint under the Third Reich as detailed as that discovered by Dr Chapman for the Weimar Republic.

The short history of the Government Code and Cypher School (GC & CS, the predecessor of today's GCHQ) by its operational head, the late Alastair Denniston, kindly made available by his son Robin, provides for the first time a general assessment of the organisation and achievements of British cryptanalysis between the wars.[7] Denniston was too modest a man to indicate how much GC & CS both between the wars and in its wartime home at Bletchley Park (which he directed until 1942) owed to his own leadership. For almost twenty years 'the little man', as he was affectionately known to his staff, succeeded in running on a shoestring a new and highly secret organisation containing a number of gifted mavericks who would not have taken kindly to a chief who worked according to bureaucratic routine and civil service hierarchy. When his resources were increased on the eve of war, he began the expansion which made possible the remarkable achievements of Bletchley Park. Just a hint of fully justified resentment at the treatment of GC & CS by its political and civil service masters is detectable in Denniston's brief history. GC & CS between the wars was, as he complains, 'an adopted child of the Foreign Office with no family rights, and the poor relation of the SIS, whose peacetime activities left little cash to spare'. Successive governments steadily jeopardised GC & CS's most striking interwar achievement – the breaking of Soviet diplomatic codes during the decade after the Bolshevik revolution – until in 1927, to Denniston's dismay, 'HMG found it necessary to compromise our work beyond any question'. Denniston's short history provides a glimpse of what historians may one day expect to find in the still forbidden archives of GC & CS. Not until those (doubtless incomplete) archives are open will historians be able to make a detailed assessment of the influence of much of GC & CS's work on British foreign and defence policy. In the meantime, however, Denniston's account indicates a number of areas for future research. The revelation, for example, that 'Only about 1935 did the French introduce any (cipher) systems which defied solution' has important implications for the history of Anglo-French relations.

Denniston's short history of GC & CS between the wars is followed by a reassessment of the birth of Ultra by Bletchley Park's most distinguished surviving cryptanalyst, Gordon Welchman. When the permanent undersecretary at the Foreign Office, Sir Alexander Cadogan, visited Bletchley Park for the first time in January 1941, he was shown round by Welchman whom he described in his diary as 'a charming young Cambridge professor'. Cadogan considered BP 'A good show' and 'Very interesting – I should like to spend a week there so as to try to understand it'. Six months later Welchman and the two other leading cryptanalysts, Alan Turing and Hugh Alexander (collectively described by Stewart Menzies, the Chief of the Secret Service, as his 'Brains Trust') were summoned to the Foreign

Office to be congratulated by Cadogan on their achievements and presented with £200 apiece.[8]

It is commonly supposed that the work of Bletchley Park consisted solely of producing Ultra intelligence by decrypting the various versions of the Enigma machine cipher. Christopher Morris's article serves as a valuable corrective to this simplistic view. He analyses for the first time the attack on some of the numerous hand ciphers employed by the Germans and the intelligence which it yielded, valuable both in its own right and for providing 'cribs' to the solution of the frequent changes in Enigma keys. Mr Morris is both a distinguished historian and a former wartime cryptographer. His career provides one example of the link between the achievements of Room 40, the main British codebreaking unit of the First World War, and those of Bletchley Park in the Second. When GC & CS began the search for wartime recruits in 1937, its chief recruiters were university dons who had worked in Room 40. 'These men,' writes Denniston in his interwar history of GC & CS, 'knew the type required.' The two most active recruiters on the eve of war were the Room 40 veterans, Frank Adcock, professor of ancient history at Cambridge and a Fellow of King's, and Frank Birch, formerly director of studies in history at King's who had left Cambridge for the stage. Christopher Morris, who was recruited by Birch, was one of twelve King's Fellows who worked at Bletchley Park.[9]

Just as Christopher Morris reminds us that wartime sigint consisted of much more than Ultra, so Roger Austin reveals the continuing importance of much older methods of message interception. The Vichy regime in wartime France used letter-opening on a massive scale both to monitor the movement of public opinion, and to detect opposition. In so doing it revived not merely the methods of military censorship during the First World War, but also a French tradition which went back to the *ancien régime* and had been further developed under the Bourbon Restoration. When Restoration governments wanted to ascertain public reaction to such events as the dissolution of the *Chambre Introuvable* in 1816, the fall of the Richelieu ministry in 1818, the assassination of the duc de Berry in 1820 and the death of Napoleon in 1821, they opened large amounts of private correspondence. As under the Vichy regime, letter-opening was used as a form of opinion poll. Parliamentary protests led the government to announce the abolition of *cabinets noirs* in 1828. In reality *cabinets noirs* continued to function, though more discreetly than before, at both the foreign ministry and the *Sûreté*. During the Second Empire letter-opening expanded once more. Victor Hugo, whose correspondence was regularly intercepted during his years in exile, used envelopes printed with the article of the penal code forbidding letter-opening. When this failed to deter the *cabinet noir*, he took to writing on the envelope 'Family matters – no need to read' – but to no effect.[10]

The work of Vichy's *Service du Contrôle Technique,* building on old royal and imperial traditions, illustrates the dependence of authoritarian regimes on message interception as an essential form of domestic intelligence gathering. Parliamentary democracies do, of course, make more limited use of the same methods to monitor 'subversion' (a term sometimes rather too broadly defined). But in authoritarian regimes where most dissent is denied access to the media and cannot be openly expressed, message interception fulfils a much more basic role. In Eastern Europe as in Vichy France it has become not merely a means of monitoring dissent but also an authoritarian substitute for opinion polls.

NOTES

1. Hankey, memo to Lloyd George, 8 Sept. 1920, House of Lords Records Office, Davidson MSS.
2. C.M. Andrew, 'Déchiffrement et diplomatie: le cabinet noir du Quai d'Orsay sous la Troisième République', *Relations Internationales,* Vol.III (1976) No.5. Idem, 'France and the German Menace', in E.R. May (ed.), *Knowing One's Enemies* (Princeton, 1985).
3. D.B.C. Lieven, *Russia and the Origins of the First World War* (London, 1983). W.C. Fuller, 'The Russian Empire' in May (ed.), *Knowing One's Enemies.*
4. Lamsdorff to Nelidov, 13 Dec. 1901, No.974; Lamsdorff to Osten-Sacken, 10 Jan. 1902, No.27, Archives du Ministère des Affaires Étrangères, Paris, Nelidov MSS. C.M. Andrew, *Théophile Delcassé and the Making of the Entente Cordiale* (London/New York, 1968), p.233.
5. Vladimir de Korostovetz, 'The Black Cabinet', *The Contemporary Review,* Vol.CLXVII (1945). David Kahn, *The Codebreakers* (London/New York, 1967), p.621. Andrew, 'Déchiffrement et diplomatie', pp.51–2.
6. C.M. Andrew, 'Codebreakers and Foreign Offices: The French, British and American Experience', in C.M. Andrew and D.N. Dilks, *The Missing Dimension* (London/Champaign, Illinois, 1984).
7. The original is now in the Churchill College Archive Centre, Cambridge.
8. Cadogan MS diary, 15 Jan., 15 July 1941, Churchill College Archive Centre, ACAD 1/10.
9. C.M. Andrew, 'F.H. Hinsley and the Cambridge Moles: Two Patterns of Intelligence Recruitment', in R. Langhorne (ed.), *Diplomacy and Intelligence during the Second World War* (Cambridge, 1985).
10. E. Vaillé, *Le cabinet noir* (Paris, 1950).

Tsarist Codebreakers and British Codes

CHRISTOPHER ANDREW and KEITH NEILSON

'I had a disagreeable shock last night which will also have its impact on you', wrote Sir Charles Hardinge, the British ambassador to Russia, to the permanent under-secretary (PUS) at the Foreign Office, Sir Thomas Sanderson, on 3 June 1904. At a formal dinner the previous evening, Hardinge had been told by a prominent Russian politician that the latter 'did not mind how much I reported in writing what he told me in conversation, but he begged me on no account to telegraph as all our telegrams are known!'[1] The British embassy had heard rumours for some time about the success of the Tsarist Foreign Ministry's *cabinet noir* in penetrating diplomatic codes. Some months before, Cecil Spring Rice, the secretary at the embassy, had written to a colleague at the Foreign Office that 'a private warning' should be given about the security of British ciphers.[2] As Hardinge admitted after receiving his 'disagreeable shock', the task of Tsarist codebreakers was simplified by the lax security of the embassy's filing system. 'I have always had my suspicions of the security of our presses,' he wrote, adding that this was crucial as '[n]aturally everybody knows that the cyphers are kept in the safe and that the key of the safe is hung in one of the presses'. His suggested solution was for him 'to have a specially secret cypher which must be kept apart from the others, of the existence of which nobody need know'. Though the secretary of state for foreign affairs, Lord Lansdowne, noted on Hardinge's letter, '[t]he cypher matter is serious. Can you suggest anything for extra secret messages?', it appears that nothing was done to deal with the security of the embassy's presses. Nor is it clear whether or not Hardinge received his own secret cipher.[3]

However, some 19 months later, in February 1906, Spring Rice wrote to the new foreign secretary, Sir Edward Grey, raising the issue of the presses again. Noting that 'with a little manipulation' the Chancery's presses could be opened, Spring Rice opined that

> Although without positive proof, traces visible on the wood of the doors and other indications give good grounds for believing that recourse has been had to this expedient to purloin archives by persons connected with the 'Cabinet Noir'.[4]

To combat this problem, Spring Rice suggested that a new press be constructed in England and shipped to the embassy.

Two weeks later, the young secretary made even more sensational allegations about the activities of the Russian authorities. In a secret despatch, he stated that '[f]or some time past papers have been abstracted from this Embassy'.[5] 'On enquiry' Spring Rice had 'established' that the papers had been stolen on the orders of a Russian secret police official, one Komissarow, who until recently had operated a secret police printing press which was used to turn out violently anti-Semitic and xenophobic tracts as part of an official clandestine campaign to bolster the autocracy against dissent. While this activity had been discontinued Komissarow still operated against the British embassy, although from his own rather than a government office.

As to the means of theft, Spring Rice was blunt. 'The porter and other persons in connection with the Embassy,' he wrote, 'are in the pay of the Police department and are also paid on delivery of papers.'[6] This latter practice was so blatant that Spring Rice reported: 'Emissaries of the police are constantly waiting in the evening outside the Embassy in order to take charge of the papers procured'. Nor was such practice confined to the British embassy, for the same occurrence was said to take place outside the American, Swedish and Belgian embassies. These embassies had been singled out for special attention, Spring Rice felt, because the Russian officials suspected that they were a means of contact for Jews and revolutionaries with their compatriots abroad.

In fact, the 'chief seat' of the activities of the Russian secret police was, Spring Rice believed, to be found abroad. He argued that the Russian police 'encourage Russians to learn English in order to obtain the post of servants in England where they will be able to continue their services to their employers'. He concluded his list of charges by suggesting that the diplomatic pouches sent throughout Russia to the various British posts as well as back to England were vulnerable and a likely target for the Russians.

Reaction at the Foreign Office was sharp. Hardinge, now returned to London as the new PUS, confirmed Spring Rice's views in a pungent minute on the latter's letter:

> The proceedings of the secret police inside the British Embassy during the past 10 months have really been a scandal &, in my opinion, the only way to put an end to it is to speak to Ct. Benckendorff [the Russian ambassador to London] in a friendly manner showing that we know perfectly well what is going on and telling him that an end must be put to such shameful proceedings. During my occupancy of the Embassy a sum of £1000 was offered to the Head Chancery servant for one cypher and he made an attempt to break open one safe in which he was detected. A letter was also

extracted at night from one of my desp.[atch] boxes by means of a false key and photographed by the secret police. I could say nothing while I was Amb' but I can now and I think it would be politic to do so before Sir A. Nicolson [Hardinge's successor as ambassador] goes to St. Petersburg.

Though Hardinge had his 'friendly' conversation with Count Benckendorff on 24 March, it appeared to have little immediate effect.

In a long, secret despatch of 12 April 1906, Spring Rice laid out the continuing problems with security which the embassy experienced.[7] In September 1904, Hardinge had discovered that a department in the Russian ministry of the interior had been established 'with a view to obtaining access to the archives of the foreign missions in St Petersburg'. Headed by a man 'who had served as chief of the Russian police at Paris', the department had managed to suborn the principal Chancery servant in the British embassy in the incident described above by Hardinge. 'Recently,' Spring Rice went on, '[d]ocuments have been supplied, which show beyond doubt, that access has been obtained to the archives of the Embassy, which have been taken off to the house of the Agent Komissarow, where they have been photographed.' This had occurred despite a new safe having been installed, the keys to the Chancery being kept at all times in the possession of the diplomatic staff and the presses being kept padlocked. The means of theft, Spring Rice deduced (from 'information which has reached me and which I am inclined to believe'), was through the agency of another bribed servant, who, Spring Rice alleged, had taken casts of the keyholes of the padlocks on the presses and been provided with duplicate keys by the Russian secret police.

Believing that the British ciphers were still secure despite the thefts which had occurred, Spring Rice took extraordinary precautions to ensure that they remained so. He slept in a room next to the Chancery with a connecting door open and kept all other entrances bolted. 'A piece of thin paper is gummed every night across the entrance fastening the door.' The suspected Chancery servant was never allowed to be in the room alone. But, as Spring Rice pointed out, 'it is not likely that this comparative immunity will be permanent'. The fact that the Russian secret police had a 'grant of 10,000 sterling for the current year' made it very likely that a successor would be found to the detected spy. The only hope for permanent relief, Spring Rice argued, was to import a 'British subject of tried character and experience' to look after the Chancery and to ensure that even this paragon was 'changed once a year or oftener'. Russians, he argued in a related despatch six weeks later, could never be trusted as the 'police are able to offer such threats and inducements' to them.[8]

When Spring Rice's despatch reached the Foreign Office, Hardinge took up the salient points with Count Benckendorff.[9] The PUS pointed out that their earlier conversation on such matters had seemingly been to no avail, but the Russian ambassador claimed that the Russian ministry of foreign affairs had been unable to act in time to prevent the occurrences detailed in Spring Rice's despatch. Benckendorff assured Hardinge that as soon as the new foreign minister, A.P. Isvolskii, was confirmed in office, 'he would write to him and insist on an end being put to them [such illicit activities]'.

The end to this series of incidents, at least so far as the documents available indicate, came in early May 1906. In a letter to Hardinge, Nicolson wrote that he would sack the suspected servant and replace him with another, trusted Russian already in the employ of one of the diplomatic staff.[10] 'This will give us time,' Nicolson told the PUS, 'to look about for a permanent Chancery servant and we can safely count upon some time elapsing before the police "nobble" him.' To aid in providing this breathing space, if not to end the Russian practice entirely, Nicolson planned to speak to Isvolskii on the subject in the hope that the actions of the secret police would be 'moderated'. Failing this, he concluded, a detective could always be brought out from England.

The efforts of the Russian secret police to penetrate the British embassy in St. Petersburg on behalf of the Tsarist *cabinet noir* during the period from 1904 to 1906 fall into a much broader pattern of both codebreaking successes and poor security in British embassies. Most successful cryptanalysis has been assisted by clues as to the contents of coded messages and/or intelligence on the code and cipher systems used. The two most successful *cabinets noirs* before the First World War, the French and the Russian, were helped by espionage. Both were able to exploit weaknesses in British embassy security. In 1891 the valet of the British ambassador in Paris, Lord Lytton, sold copies of diplomatic telegrams to French military intelligence.[11] Half a century later British embassy security was still sometimes woefully defective. Before the Second World War a Chancery servant in the Rome embassy gave the Italians regular access to secret documents in the ambassador's safe. In 1943–44 the valet of the British ambassador in Ankara performed a similar service for the Germans. Not until the Second World War did the Foreign Office appoint its first unpaid security adviser, and not until after the war did it set up a small security department. Positive vetting for all diplomatic staff was introduced only after the flight of Burgess and Maclean in 1951.[12]

During the first half of the twentieth century the Foreign Office tended to react with short-term alarm to revelations of lapses in British security and then to relapse into over-confidence once the immediate crisis was past. Thus it was after the 'disagreeable shocks' in St. Petersburg of

1904–06. The embassy's belief in 1906 that its ciphers were still secure was probably mistaken. Within a year Sir Francis Bertie, the British ambassador in Paris, discovered that the *cabinet noir* at the Quai d'Orsay was able to decrypt his telegrams. 'The cypher book used,' he reported, 'was suppressed.' Over the next few years Bertie's optimism about British code and cipher security returned. He wrote in May 1911:

> I know on good authority that there is more difficulty at the Quai d'Orsay in decyphering the Russian and English official cypher than those of other nationalities because the Russian and ours are changed oftener than those of other countries viz new ones made I suppose.[13]

So far as the Russian *cabinet noir* was concerned, however, Bertie's confidence in British ciphers was misplaced. Tsarist diplomatic documents published by the Bolsheviks between the wars show that the *cabinet noir* was able to decrypt a probably substantial amount of British diplomtic traffic both up to and beyond the outbreak of war. During the year before the war Russian cryptanalysts had significant success with the code and ciphers of all the great powers save Germany[14] whose systems were substantially improved after revelations that their telegrams had been read by the French during the Agadir crisis of 1911.[15] After the outbreak of war the Russians found the ease with which they could decrypt their British and French allies' traffic something of an embarrassment. The British intelligence officer (and future foreign secretary), Sir Samuel Hoare, was warned in 1916 by a Russian official to change his ciphers since his existing ones could be read as easily as a 'newspaper'.[16]

With the outbreak of war, however, the Tsarist *cabinet noir* became an ally as well as a rival. The main British cryptanalytical agency of the First World War, Room 40 at the Admiralty, owed its first success in breaking German naval codes to the gift from the Russians in October 1914 of the *Signalbuch der Kaiserlichen Marine,* captured after the sinking of a German cruiser in the Baltic.[17] After the October Revolution of 1917 an even more remarkable alliance was formed between British and Tsarist cryptanalysis. The Bolshevik seizure of power was followed by the dispersion of many of the Tsarist codebreakers. One of the ablest, E.C. Fetterlein, escaped to England in 1918 and became head of the Russian section at the British interwar cryptanalytical agency, GC & CS. The great American codebreaker, William Friedman, who met Fetterlein at the end of the war, later wrote of him:

> ... I vividly recall that he wore with great pride on the index finger of his right hand a ring in which was mounted a largy ruby. When I showed interest in this unusual gem, he told me that the ring had

been presented to him as a token of recognition and thanks for his cryptanalytic successes while in the service of Czar Nicholas, the last of the line.

Ironically, those successes had included decrypting British diplomatic traffic.[18] Some of the skills employed by the Tsarist *cabinet noir* against British codes were thus used by the British after the Bolshevik Revolution to break Soviet codes. The cabinet secretary, Maurice Hankey, wrote to the prime minister after one success by GC & CS against Soviet traffic in 1920:

> This particular cypher is a very ingenious one which was discovered by great cleverness and hard work. The key to the cypher is changed daily and sometimes as often as three times in one message ... You will recall that the Russians were the first to introduce us to this system of de-coding, and I believe one of our most skilful experts [Fetterlein] was and is of Russian origin.[19]

Thanks in large measure to Fetterlein and the accumulated expertise of the Tsarist *cabinet noir*, the most valuable diplomatic intelligence source available to the British intelligence services during the decade after the Bolshevik Revolution was the decrypted traffic of the Soviet government.[20]

NOTES

Keith Neilson would like to thank the Social Sciences and Humanities Research Council of Canada for a Leave Fellowship which made possible part of the research upon which this article is based.

1. Hardinge to Sanderson, 3 June 1904, private, Lansdowne Papers, FO 800/115. All papers in the FO series cited in these notes are in the Public Record Office, Kew.
2. Spring Rice to Louis Mallet, 29 Oct. 1903, Lansdowne Papers, FO 800/140.
3. Minute by Lansdowne on Hardinge to Sanderson, note 1 above. Sanderson noted enigmatically on this letter, 'There is an explanation. See minute [illegible] June 11'. We have not found this minute.
4. Spring Rice to Grey, 12 Feb. 1906, despatch 121, FO 371/123/5945.
5. Spring Rice to Grey, 28 Feb. 1906, secret despatch 151, FO 371/123/7670.
6. Ibid. In a marginal minute on this point, Hardinge noted that 'Though probable there is no proof of this, I believe'.
7. Spring Rice to Grey, 12 April 1906, secret despatch 263, FO 371/123/12817.
8. Spring Rice to Grey, 28 May 1906, despatch 332, FO 371/123/19845.
9. Memorandum by Hardinge of a conversation with Benckendorff, 9 May 1906, FO 371/123/16723.
10. Nicolson to Hardinge, 4 May 1906, FO 371/123/19845.
11. M. Paleologue, *Journal de l'affaire Dreyfus 1894-1899* (Paris, 1955), pp.43-5. C.M. Andrew, 'Déchiffrement et diplomatie: le cabinet noir du Quai d'Orsay sous la Troisième République', *Relations Internationales*, Vol.III (1976), No.5, pp.45, 50-1.
12. C.M. Andrew and D.N. Dilks (eds.), *The Missing Dimension: Government and Intelligence Communities in the Twentieth Century* (London, 1984), pp.106-18, 181-2.

13. Bertie to Nicolson, 7 May 1911, Nicolson Papers, FO 800/348. Bertie recalled the discovery that the French had broken British ciphers as taking place 'four or five years ago'.
14. See, for example, the numerous intercepts in the four series of Russian documents in German translation edited by Otto Hoetzch, *Die Internationalen Beziehungen im Zeitalter des Imperialismus* (Berlin, 1933–42). This collection includes only samples of intercepted material from which it is impossible to judge the total amount available to the Russian foreign ministry. The latest German intercept published is for 1912.
15. Andrew, 'Déchiffrement et diplomatie', pp.53–5.
16. Sir Samuel Hoare, *The Fourth Seal* (London, 1930), p.57. See also Keith Neilson, '"Joy Rides?" British Intelligence and Propaganda in Russia, 1914–1917', *Historical Journal*, Vol.XXIV (1981), No.4; and Vladimir de Korostovetz, 'The Black Cabinet', *The Contemporary Review*, Vol.CLXVII (1945).
17. On Room 40 see Patrick Beesly, *Room 40* (London, 1982) and C.M. Andrew, *Secret Service: The Making of the British Intelligence Community* (London, 1985), Ch.3.
18. W.F. Friedman, 'Six Lectures on Cryptography', April 1963, p.118, National Archives, Washington, RG 457 SRH-004. Cf the references to Fetterlein in the article by A.G. Denniston below.
19. Hankey, memo to Lloyd George, 8 Sept. 1920, House of Lords Record Office, Davidson Papers.
20. Andrew, *Secret Service*, Chs.9, 10.

No Final Solution: A Survey of the Cryptanalytical Capabilities of German Military Agencies, 1926–35

J.W.M. CHAPMAN

The anecdotal evidence available from reported statements of twentieth-century decision-makers about the influence of covert intelligence over policy formation suggests a sharp dichotomy between the gullible and the contumaciously dismissive. Many of the latter instances appear to refer most pointedly to agent information as either naive or motivated by personal gain. Hitler provides a classic example of the second school of intuitive thinking, as evidenced from the case of the 'swindler' operating inside the Soviet mission in Berlin in 1941.[1] His views on the subject had evidently hardened by 1943, when he was reported as retorting that 'such people should be shot' on having the case of another agent working against the Soviet Union brought to his attention.[2] Signals intelligence, on the other hand, could not be so readily discredited, even by former inhabitants of the Central European demi-monde. His foreign minister, Ribbentrop, who can be numbered among the gullible, complained somewhat bitterly to his American interrogators in 1945 that his leader was being briefed, particularly about Anglo-American matters, by sources unavailable to him.[3] If Hitler had thought so little of those who dealt with high-level intelligence, he would scarcely have arranged for the liquidation of Generals von Schleicher and von Bredow in June 1934, whose inside knowledge of the Nazi Party had been so heavily dependent on covert intelligence-gathering for a decade prior to its accession to power.[4]

A reconstruction from the historical evidence of the precise nature and significance of covertly derived intelligence in relation to policy formation is greatly hampered not just by the sensitivity of the relevant written evidence and its concomitant proneness to destruction or concealment, but also by the perpetual motion of organisational change designed to draw discreet veils over the operation of covert agencies. Such problems are common to all national policymaking systems at every period, and this makes it extremely difficult to appraise with any real precision either the influence of the 'missing dimension' in general, or that of any one branch of it, such as signals intelligence, in particular.[5] Added to this set of problems for the historian is the even more daunting task of seeking to appraise the value of the cryptological dimension comparatively across the national decision-making units in order to evaluate any system-determining inputs into the international system of the relevant era.

In saying this, one should at the same time be very careful to avoid building in any assumption that any single factor or actor may have played a predetermining role. On the other hand, there is the opposite trap of assuming that systemic structures predetermined the behaviour of either individual national units or national intelligence–gathering apparatuses. Professor Medlicott's question about whether the nineteenth-century Concert of Europe shaped the long period of comparative peace in Europe, or whether it was the peace that provided the vital preconditions for the operation of the Concert remains as pertinent to systems theorising as the epigram of Professor Locher that

> One should not confuse totality with completeness. The whole is more than the assembled parts, but it is also surely less.[6]

The evidence about covert intelligence agencies is far from, and far from likely ever to be, complete. Fresh discoveries are constantly reported about national systems, and attention is drawn in the present article to the cryptanalytical activities of German military agencies in the 1920s and 1930s mainly to add to the body of comparative data available. Its value is comparatively high-grade, if for no other reason than that the archival evidence includes a continuous set of quarterly logs submitted to the Chief of the Secret Military Intelligence Group in the General Staff (transferred to the Defence Minister's Secretariat from April 1928) that summarise, in a more comprehensive way than most, German cryptanalytical activities for the period from October 1925 to December 1933.[7] Another feature of the material is that it illuminates the role of signals intelligence in peacetime and contrasts the different priorities that arise in comparison with its operational role in the First and Second World Wars, on which the literature is so much more prolific and eloquent.[8] A large gap still remains to be filled for the period from 1933 to 1939, a period that can be characterised as 'neither peace nor war', to borrow the phrase used by the late Hugh Seton-Watson about our own era, and which was covered so tantalisingly briefly in the official British history by Professor Hinsley.[9] Nevertheless, a background awareness of the parallel developments taking place among the different national systems is a constant check to the ever present possibilities of falling into the reductionist trap so prominently featured in the critical work of Professor Waltz.[10]

THE TECHNOLOGICAL AND ECONOMIC SETTINGS

Any discussion of wholes and parts that relate to the 'modern world-system' cannot readily ignore the pervasive and dynamic role of scientific and technological developments on the political, military and economic structures on which that system is heavily, though not exclusively, based. The late Professor Barraclough argued for the emergence of a 'scientific revolution' in the final quarter of the nineteenth century and the information technology on which today's tertiary industries are increasingly based manifestly is not only rooted in that 'revolution', but its earlier applications provided the cybernetic basis for the growth of signals and electronic intelligence in the first place. The past century has undoubtedly witnessed the steady institutionalisation of a system of scientific research and development that has its own internal logic and dynamic, perhaps even laws, which interacts closely with all other social systems and appears to operate in a fashion not so dissimilar to the anonymous economic market. Its allegedly self-regulating mechanisms give it the model qualities identified by Professor Deutsch in cybernetic systems as a salient characteristic of the post-mechanical age, in sharp contrast with the cruder imagery of the balance of power.[11]

What is certain, at any rate, is that most of the techniques of interception of communications had already emerged before the First World War, but it was during wartime that technological developments in electronic means of communication and experience of their interception had markedly increased in the belligerent states.[12] The post-war German Army and Naval Commands retained substantial signals departments which maintained close links with the expanding industrial firms such as Telefunken, Lorenz, and Siemens, engaged in research and development in their own establishments and also benefited from research undertaken in civilian ministries and the universities. The military provided contracts for the industrial firms and also contacts with foreign military establishments with which the German armed forces had collaborative arrangements. Most of the pre-war German cable network overseas was lost, but the possibilities for the establishment of a world-wide network of German radio transmitters were identified by Admiral Kurt Zenker, a subsequent chief of the Naval Command, as early as March 1919:

> The creation of a wireless network covering all the main trade routes for world shipping is of decisive importance for us. In our unfortunate maritime position, our cable links can be cut off very easily every time a war breaks out, so that we would do well to concentrate on wireless. The importance of a secure signals service has been adequately demonstrated in the course of the war and the fact that it has as good as completely broken down was fatal for us.

Aside from the construction of major stations under German control, we must strive for their construction in the colonies of friendly states overseas by German companies and ensure their servicing by German personnel so that we can create a rapid signals service independent of England, which, apart from their important peacetime purposes, would undertake to warn and support our merchant shipping in times when the threat of war was imminent.

The erection of such stations must be attempted:
1) for the Atlantic Ocean: in Mexico and Argentina;
2) for the Indian Ocean: in Goa (Portuguese India), and on Sumatra and Java;
3) for the South Seas and the Pacific Ocean: in the event of the elimination of all German colonies: in Dutch New Guinea or Portuguese Timor, in China and Chile (possibly also on Easter Island).[13]

Along with other expectations dashed soon thereafter by the publication of the terms of the Versailles Treaty, these proposals had largely to be shelved until better days. Zenker maintained good connections with German enterprises abroad between 1924 and 1928, and German transmitters were eventually installed in the Spanish Atlantic islands, Brazil and Thailand, among others at this period, while the German army developed links in Russia, South America and China for the sale and testing of radio communications for military and aviation purposes.

The radio industry blossomed in the inter-war period and some three million home receivers were registered in Germany by 1930. Technical developments were very rapid and the German manufacturing industry was helped by the relatively liberal cross-licensing arrangements among European and American producers and by the fact that American giants such as ITT acquired a stake in the German telecommunications industry as part of an early American direct investment drive in the new wave of industries in Europe.[14] The German field army was equipped with mobile transmitters by the late 1920s, but most of the commercial radio traffic abroad was handled by public transmitters such as that at Nauen, which had been in operation since the war.

German diplomatic traffic was almost entirely carried by postal cable until 1935, when the first transmitter was installed in the German mission at Addis Ababa during the Italo-Ethiopian conflict.[15] This development stemmed directly from the dramatic improvements in short-wave transmission. These were also of importance to the German navy, which had begun to send its fleet units on training cruises to all the world's oceans from 1925, and needed to test the reliability of its equipment for secure communications with the homeland. A few of the more modern German merchant shipping fleets had also installed radio equipment on board their vessels. In 1928, arrangements were made for naval codebooks (Code E) to be issued to warships for communication with German consular posts abroad, but it was not until the mid 1930s that arrangements had been made to issue a merchant ship code (Code H) to the shipping lines for use in the event of the outbreak of an international crisis or hostilities involving Germany.[16]

Short-wave transmitters were also secretly issued to German military attachés in several European capitals without the knowledge of the German Foreign Ministry. Subsequently, however, agreements were reached between the Secret Service and the Foreign Ministry in 1936 for collaboration in this area, and a joint testing programme was carried out with low-power transmitters from missions in Helsinki and Istanbul as part of preparations in readiness for the outbreak of war. By 1939, most diplomatic missions abroad had been supplied with military short-wave sets, and an agreement was arrived at in March 1940 for joint use under Foreign Ministry supervision. The Secret Service also equipped its agents in neutral, as well as enemy countries with low-powered sets independently of Foreign Ministry efforts at controlling the communication systems of the armed forces.[17]

During the 1920s, the armed forces developed the commercial versions of the 'Enigma' ciphering machines for military use. As is well known, different models with varying numbers of rotors were developed and supplied to all the armed forces and the internal security agencies. In 1936, the German naval attaché in Sweden provided the Swedish inventor, Carl Hagelin, with introductions to the Naval and War Ministry cryptographic Sections. But Hagelin's efforts to sell his equipment to the Germans came to nothing, apparently because this was already being supplied to the French and because the German side thought that their existing equipment was superior to that of the Swedes.[18] At least one example of an American cipher machine was captured in North Africa in early 1943, and study of this convinced the German navy at least that it was 'substantially inferior to our own equipment in terms of its resistance to decipherment'.[19] Since American machine ciphers proved virtually impossible for the Germans to decipher, it added to the strength of the German conviction that a systematic reading of their ciphers by the enemy powers was out of the question and that losses in suspicious circumstances must be due to unseen reconnaissance, espionage or treason rather than cipher insecurity.

Machine ciphers, however, tended to be used rather sparingly for traffic outside Germany before 1939. Codebooks and occasionally machines disappeared with disturbing frequency in the 1920s, and front-line units had to practise use of cipher machines for training purposes, especially during manoeuvres, but training manuals of the late 1930s emphasised that lack of tight control in the use of ciphering procedures was tantamount to treason and the penalties for such misdemeanours became increasingly draconian from 1934.[20]

Attachés abroad generally operated mechanical ciphers until machines were issued as standard following the outbreak of war. In 1935, attachés were also warned of the dangers of listening devices in their offices and living quarters abroad after the Hungarian Secret Service briefed its German counterparts in the technical advances it had made with such equipment since the 1920s. The Cipher Section (*C-Stelle*) had issued such warnings at least as early as 1928, and a German firm was named as a supplier of such devices to the Soviet Trade Mission in Berlin, the Polish authorities, and the Hungarian military attaché.[21]

THE CENTRALISED DECIPHERMENT SERVICE

Command and Control

Data about the General Staff's system of organisation before 1925 appear to be sparse, though there are some details of training manuals in signals and monitoring for the period 1900 to 1925. The General Staff in Germany organised the covert intelligence-gathering side of its activities along the conventional lines of the day, with both non-covert and covert aspects under the roof of the Intelligence Section (*T3*). Liaison was maintained with the equivalent signals group in the Signals Section of the Naval Command (*AIII*), which contained only a small group of decipherers and was separate from the Fleet Section (*AII*) where non-covert, covert and counter-intelligence was assembled by separate desk experts. Between 1926 and 1928, the German press managed to get hold of damaging evidence about the German army's covert activities in the Soviet Union and also about the links between naval intelligence and rightist extremist groups, much of which was divulged in the *Reichstag* as part of the Social Democratic Party's bid for return to power in the central government coalition.[22]

General Groener, who had signed the early agreement with the Social Democratic leader, Friedrich Ebert, to restore order in the country in the wake of the mutinies and collapse in 1918, was brought in to 'clean up' the Defence Ministry in 1928. An important part of this process lay in curtailing the activities of the military and naval intelligence agencies and the growing signs of their activities abroad, which the Foreign Ministry viewed with some alarm and which led to demarcation disputes with diplomatic representatives abroad. Groener promoted a former protégé, Colonel Kurt von Schleicher, to be his *chef de cabinet* and ordered that all covert intelligence activity by both army and navy be brought under the control of a centralised Secret Military Intelligence Section directly subordinate to the minister's secretariat at the end of March 1928. What von Schleicher proposed, giving a mere fortnight for the implementation of these directives, was a wholesale transfer of the covert (espionage and decipherment) and counter-intelligence activities of the two services and for them to be merged under a single roof. Since the concept was based on von Schleicher's intimate knowledge of army practice, having served as its expert on domestic political intelligence for many years, it did comparatively little to disrupt the army's establishment. But the very much smaller naval establishment found such proposals highly disruptive to its intelligence organisation, and resistance to the changes was stout, especially as efforts had been made to reorganise and decentralise in the wake of the exposures in both 1927 and 1928. What was particularly objectionable in the navy's eyes was the proposal to truncate its centralised decipherment and radio monitoring set-up, which experience in the World War had shown was vital to fleet operations and was even more vital in the contemporary situation where the navy could not afford to lose a single warship in the face of Franco-Polish encirclement.[23]

The upshot of this dispute was that a small number of the less important naval intelligence desks (counter-espionage, the World Intelligence Service, and newly refounded Naval Supply Organisation) were transferred to the Defence Ministry, and a fresh directive was issued by von Schleicher excluding the navy's monitoring and deciphering service (*B-*

FIGURE 1
ORGANISATION CHART OF THE SECRET MILITARY INTELLIGENCE
SECTION (ABWEHR) IN THE GERMAN MINISTRY OF DEFENCE, 1928

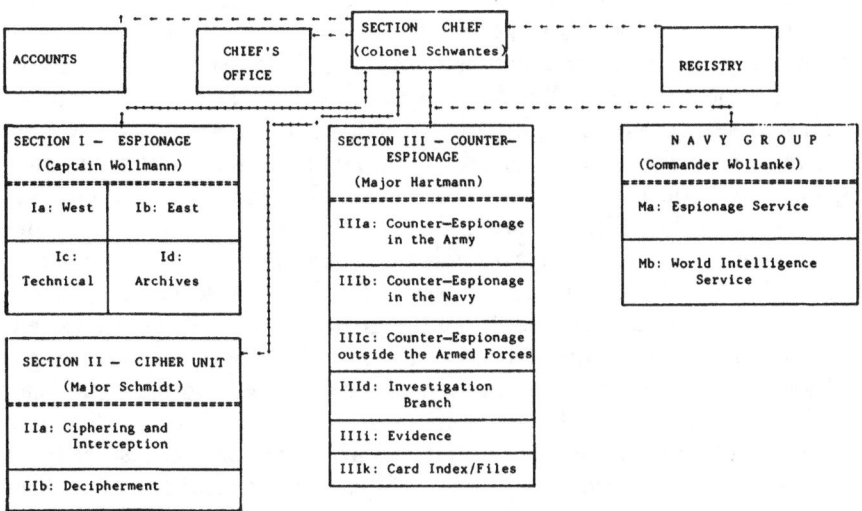

Dienst) from the new arrangements. Nevertheless, given the tighter control exercised over the naval budget by the Defence Ministry, it seems that this service was denied funds requested for the appointment of personnel to handle Polish and Soviet naval cipher material, ostensibly on the ground that the central Decipherment Section (*E-Stelle*) already had adequate staff for the purpose and would continue to handle intercepts passed on to it from naval monitoring posts as in the past. That the quarrel ran quite deep may be gauged by the fact that at the functional level, the navy was left off the distribution list of the Decipherment Section's circulars for a period of 18 months in 1929–30 and the World Intelligence Service was axed by the defence minister in line with the wishes of the Foreign Ministry in June 1929.[24] The navy appears to have responded by transferring the *B-Dienst* from Naval Signals in Berlin to Kiel, where it was temporarily concealed under the control of Rear-Admiral Junkermann, the inspector of mines and torpedoes, who also happened to be responsible for research on underwater acoustics in connection with countering anti-submarine warfare.[25] The dispute also coincided with the departure of Admiral Zenker as chief of the naval command and of his chief of staff, Rear Admiral Pfeiffer, and with the appointment of the long-serving Erich Raeder, while Lieutenant-Colonel von Bredow came in to replace Colonel Schwantes as head of the Secret Service in 1929.

Von Bredow appears to have been a much more politically aware and involved officer than Schwantes, who had replaced Gempp, the compiler of the history of the Secret Service up to 1918.[26] He undoubtedly sought to improve the links of the new service with other agencies, notably with the police and civilian ministries involved in internal security, and also especially with the Foreign Ministry, which was eventually won round to the appointment of military attachés abroad and to a measure of co-operation with the revised Naval Supply Organisation, which in turn partly made up to the navy for his earlier appeasement of the Foreign Ministry's demands for the abolition of the World Intelligence Service. The latter organisation had served as something of a model for a proposal advanced by Admiral Behncke for a combined military, political and economic intelligence service on a global scale to Chancellor Bruening in 1931 not unlike the contemporary CIA in the United States. Any ambitions that von Bredow may have had in this direction were abruptly halted by the fall of von Schleicher from office in January 1933. His naval successors, Patzig and Canaris, increasingly deplored the growth of Nazi Party-sponsored intelligence organisations abroad and sought the support of the Foreign Ministry and others for the creation of a centralised foreign espionage service to be headed by Hitler's deputy, Hess.[27] Not only did such a plan come to nothing, but the Secret Military Intelligence Service lost the bulk of its Cipher Section to Armed Forces Signals in reorganisations of 1936 and 1938, having already lost numbers of personnel to Goering's *Forschungsamt* in the summer of 1933.[28]

Structurally speaking, both the Secret Military Intelligence Service and the Decipherment Section were superstructures dependent on subordinate infrastructures controlled by separate organisations. Despite what the highest officials in state and government might decree from above, their personnel were subject to transfer at regular intervals, and the promotion of ordinary personnel serving temporarily with these bodies depended on the services which seconded them in the first place. The Decipherment Section, for example, depended quite vitally on army and navy radio monitoring posts for the supply of much of its raw materials and for corroboration of any signals it itself intercepted. This dependence was underlined in a memorandum of October 1931:

> A precondition for identifying and maximising all the compromising elements without any exceptions that would permit the unauthorised decipherment of foreign codes lies in a careful and painstakingly accurate interception of cables. This is the physical basis for unauthorised decipherment. Without such a precondition, the fruits of decipherment, no matter what the exactitude of all available methods or of the preparedness for employing these, could only ripen but slowly, or indeed so late that the harvest would be spoiled even before it ripened.[29]

Co-ordination of Decipherment Activities

The fact that the Naval Command could evade the controls that Berlin sought to impose on its decipherment activities when it was a much weaker organisation than the Army Command is eloquent testimony of the need for co-ordination and co-operation from the very inception of efforts at command and control which proved ineffective. Eventually the navy's small team, working mainly on British and French ciphers and almost wholly unsuccessfully on Italian ciphers, returned to the fold, and collaborative relations were resumed. Work was also eventually extended to Polish and Soviet naval ciphers with a small degree of success. Greater co-operation with both the navy and the Foreign Ministry depended very heavily on von Schleicher's ability to convince them of the need to collaborate on grounds of national security (*Landesschutz*) against an alleged threat along Germany's long, open frontier with Poland, whose past behaviour and pretensions were universally condemned by all sections of German political opinion. The external Polish threat was inevitably linked with French encirclement strategies and elaborate operational planning exercises, training and manoeuvres were built round this central issue. But it was an issue that conjoined in the years from 1930 to 1933 with growing domestic unrest inside Germany itself and spectres were increasingly raised of a Polish seizure of Danzig and East Prussia if ever domestic turmoil should reach a pitch where the police and the armed forces proved unequal to the maintenance of law and order.

Similarly elaborate operational plans were drawn up to cope with a domestic crisis or civil war, which entailed collaboration among central and local government agencies, a stance that was met with manifest reluctance on the part of regions like Prussia controlled by Social Democrat administrations, which were subjected to the pains of defenestration in the summer of 1932. As part of this co-ordination in the name of national security, arrangements were made for the various military and civilian agencies involved in the surveillance of communications to draw up regulations for their control in the event of an emergency in the guise of a sub-committee of the National Defence Council (*RVA*). This was notionally controlled by the Cabinet, but it was effectively a device for enabling the aged and increasingly enfeebled president to delegate rule by decree to the army. The sub-committee was headed by Lieutenant-Colonel Erich Fellgiebel, subsequently involved in a not dissimilar plot to remove Hitler from office in 1944. The Council's secretary was Captain Schmundt of the Organisation Section of the General Staff (*T2*), but the drafting of the complex emergency plans as a whole brought a certain Major Wilhelm Keitel to the fore, and in his train a certain Captain Alfred Jodl.[30] In 1935, Keitel succeeded to the post of *chef de cabinet* to the war minister, first occupied by von Schleicher, while Jodl was installed as head of the National Security Section (*Abteilung Landesverteidigung*).

Fellgiebel had served briefly with the Decipherment Section before being appointed army inspector-general of signals and can hardly have failed to be privy to the arrangements for the monitoring of internal as well as external communications. At a domestic level, it certainly involved telephone taps on party political organisations, including the Nazi Party, but probably also extended to the president's offices and those of members of the Cabinet. A memorandum of April 1930 confirms that the Secret Military Intelligence Service was supplied with listening devices by the Visophon Company, and that other consumers included the Berlin magistrates and the criminal police employed by the national railways.[31] By 1936, expertise in and control of the deployment of these kinds of monitoring device had visibly shifted to the Gestapo, despite the fact that Defence Minister von Blomberg had managed to get Hitler to agree in writing on 24 October 1933 to his ministry having the authority to issue guidelines to central and local government agencies for 'all steps necessary for the protection of national security and in the defence policy sphere in the areas of counter-espionage and propaganda'.[32]

By the spring of 1934, the emergency regulations had been made to work in favour of the ruling Nazi Party. The third draft of the regulations covering 'The Surveillance of Communications' was subtly amended to bring matters into line with current political reality. For example, the previous references to 'military surveillance' of communications was now not held to mean that only soldiers had to be involved. Responsibility for the monitoring of radio broadcasts was now to be transferred to the *Forschungsamt*, while checks on German press and radio were to be the responsibility of the Propaganda Ministry. Even the communication links of the Economics Ministry with foreign countries were to be the responsibility of the Foreign Ministry.[33] Even the stigmatisation of Poland as the key enemy state had now been superseded. Hitler pursued a policy of *détente* with Poland that had been crowned by the Non-Aggression Pact of January 1934 and the Soviet Union replaced Poland as the national *bête noire*. Emergency planning correspondingly shifted away from the domestic sphere to operational planning for war with France and the Soviet Union, though the encirclement image remained firmly at the forefront of Hitler's foreign policy concerns. The Secret Service under Captain Patzig, however, tended to respond rather slowly to the reorientation in German foreign policy, even though army officers in its employ had for a long time continued to maintain friendly relations with various Russian emigré groups living in Central Europe and with states like Finland, Lithuania, Hungary and Austria which were apprehensive about the Soviet threat, but not tied very closely to the Western Powers.[34] A more dynamic change came with the appointment of Wilhelm Canaris, who not only strengthened existing links with these states, but also sought to draw states formerly in the Western orbit, such as Latvia, Estonia, Turkey, Spain, Japan, Italy and even Poland, into Hitler's anti-Soviet and anti-communist league.

At the working level, the military cryptanalysts attached to the Secret Service continued to maintain informal relations with former military officers employed by other agencies, such as Senior Counsellor Selchow of the Foreign Ministry, and Major von Wrochem of the Propaganda Ministry. Official liaison officers were appointed with the Ministry of Posts (Lieutenant-Colonel Dohne), and the Air Ministry (First Lieutenant Flesch and retired Colonel Lindner), while rather more wary relations were maintained with the *Forschungsamt* (retired Commander Schimpf and retired Captain Schapper). The transfer of six deciphering specialists, including Major Seifert, to the *Forschungsamt* in 1933 was privately regarded as an act of disloyalty to the Deciphering Section.[35] The previous co-operation that had existed with the Police Presidium in Berlin and with the old political police (*Reichskommissariat für Überwachung der öffentlichen Ordnung*) appears to have sunk with very little trace after 1933.[36]

Overseas Network Analysis

The relationship with the Ministry of Posts was particularly important bcause of the need to obtain copies of encoded diplomatic and consular cablegrams and radiograms passing along German-controlled communication channels. Germany, it should not be forgotten, lay at the centre of European rail, air, cable and telephone networks on both a north–south axis (Stockholm–Naples) and an east–west axis (Istanbul–Moscow–London–Lisbon), with connections to the Middle and Far East and the Americas. While this fact made it less necessary for the German authorities themselves to depend on extensive radio communications abroad, it made it easier for their radio monitoring stations to pick up the signals of other states which relied more heavily on overseas radio networks. The European states with colonies overseas, for example, were increasingly dependent in this way, and particular attention was paid to British military and diplomatic traffic with the Middle East, India and the Far East, French traffic with Africa, the Near East and Indochina, and Italian traffic to Africa and the Middle East. In addition, the Soviet authorities needed extensive radio networks for relations between the centre and various parts of their vast country: not only armed forces and diplomatic traffic was intercepted, radio stations used by internal security forces and later by the collective farms were monitored, together with the various Comintern channels. Another important radio user was the United States, where both the State and War Departments employed radiograms with growing frequency in traffic with continental Europe.

Figure 2 indicates the location of the main army and navy listening posts round the periphery of German territory. The central Decipherment Section and its own listening posts were in the Berlin area, while the navy's *B-Dienst* functioned either in Berlin or Kiel, with listening posts dotted along the sea coasts of the Baltic and North Seas, which could always be used in conjunction with warships and other vessels at sea.[37] Army listening posts were located mainly in fixed radio stations close to command posts in the military districts and linked to field posts close to the frontier, so that information derived from traffic analysis could be passed on to local commanders and army signals headquarters. The listening post at Münster, for example, concentrated on British radio signals and its work was supplemented by navy posts. Stuttgart monitored French radio transmissions, Munich Italian, Breslau Czech and Balkan traffic, but sometimes assisted Frankfurt-on-Oder (and later Jüterbog) or Königsberg with Polish transmissions, though Königsberg was mainly concerned with Soviet networks.

All section heads in the Secret Service in the 1920s and 1930s were required to submit quarterly reports of sectional activities, of which a full set has survived for the Decipherment Section for the period from Octo-

FIGURE 2
GERMAN SIGNALS INTELLIGENCE NETWORK, 1933

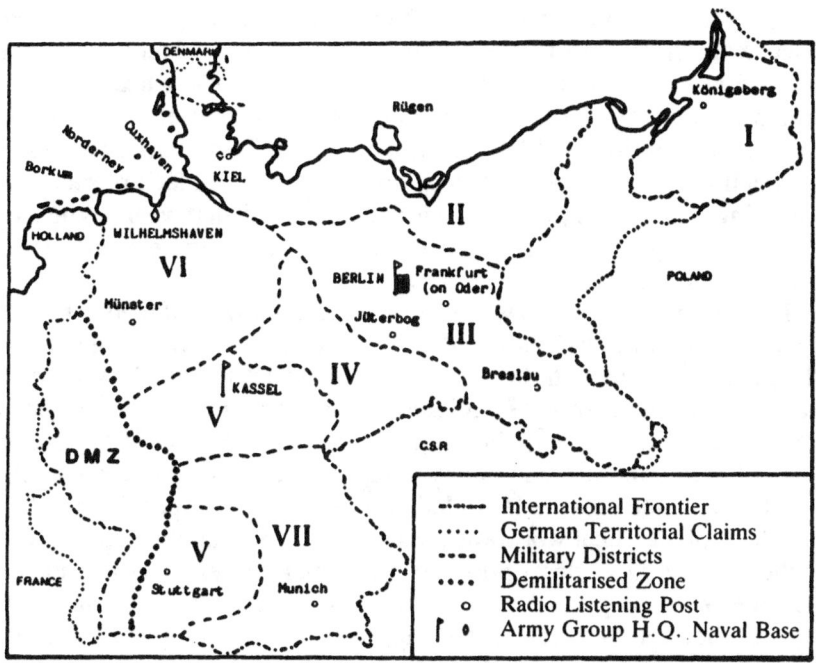

ber 1925 to the end of December 1933. These generally represent a more comprehensive and continuous survey of cryptanalytical activities than the comparable archival materials for most other contemporary states, which have normally allowed only low-level and disconnected or stray items on decipherment to reach public scrutiny, though such materials can sometimes be found in private diaries or papers, not always subjected to official weeding. Apart from the indications given to superiors about the amount of work throughput, areas of special concentration and successes achieved, these reports indicate a good deal of statistical evidence over time. They do not appear to have been compiled for statistical purposes, however, as they only once indicate the total number of signals intercepted: some 117,000 in the calendar year 1927, and only 2.8 per cent of this raw input was converted into deciphered clear-texts submitted to military intelligence evaluation agencies.

Figure 3 provides a summary of statistical data gleaned from the quarterly reports for a full eight-year period. The second column indicates the numbers of ciphers logged, which included peripheral European states and independent states in the Americas and Asia, none of which was systematically analysed at this period, with the exception of the United States. The proportion of cryptographs analysed to those logged varied between one-quarter and one-third. Relative success rates can be judged from column three, while the contributions in terms of end products from the central Decipherment Section and the listening posts can be assessed in column 4. The annual number of clear-texts, listed in column 6, shows the relative work-rate over the whole period. Significant dips can be identified in 1930–31 and a clear correlation can be established between the low numbers of clear-texts and the total lack of success in resolving any new ciphers during the winter of that year. When the numbers of signals are very high, the success rate with new and concurrent resolutions rises exponentially.

The quarterly reports, which were occasionally conflated into half-yearly ones, normally contained an introductory overview summarising the progress made with the codes and ciphers of individual countries by name. They then went on to identify the different circuits logged by geographical area: East, Baltic States, Balkans, South, West, North, Asia, Africa, America and finally news agencies and commercial traffic. The third section provided detailed information on the specific circuits on which cryptanalytical work was taking place. This mainly involved quite elaborate technical descriptions of particular ciphers, the methods of decipherment employed and information on the construction of the ciphers themselves. Occasionally, appendices were compiled about specially difficult codes or ciphers successfully broken, which indicated innovations of technique or other special features.

The first section appears to have been the one of special interest to the layman within the higher echelons of the military hierarchy. The top copy was normally submitted to the Chief of the Secret Military Intelligence Service, but few top copies appear to have survived and those that did were usually initialled and particular sections of current interest marked in the margins. There are very few pencilled comments in the margins and these are mostly by archival clerks. One copy was normally sent to the Naval Command for information and the remaining copies retained by both the Deciphering Group (*Abwehr IIb*) and the East European desk in the Ciphering Group (*IIa*). This suggests that the reports were mainly of value to the technical deciphering specialists in the Defence Ministry and also to their own cipher specialists as a means for keeping the German side abreast of the latest developments and to incorporate any lessons observed in the decipherment of foreign traffic in increased German cipher security. It is clear from later evidence of the 1930s and 1940s that the Ciphering Group was asked to test the security of German military ciphers by the military agencies concerned, but it also scrutinised the codes and ciphers of other agencies unbidden: for example, those of the

GERMAN CRYPTANALYTICAL CAPABILITIES, 1926–35

FIGURE 3

YEAR/QUARTER		CODES & CIPHERS LOGGED	CODES & CIPHERS ANALYSED	RESOLUTIONS CONCURRENT*	RESOLUTIONS NEW*	+ SUPERENCIPHERMENTS	CLEAR-TEXTS SUBMITTED FOR EVALUATION (1)	(2)	@ (3)	ANNUAL TOTAL
1926	Q1	85	22	16	6		135	240	143	
	Q2	94	28	17	6		163	184	375	
	Q3	92	24	14	5		306	205	347	
	Q4	90	23	18					511	1,376
1927	Q1	90	25	20	6	125	427	312	739	
	Q2	101	29	22	5	168	506	403	909	
	Q3	117	29	20	3	175	342	381	723	
	Q4	110	29	18	3		579	381	960	3,331
1928	Q1	107	32	24	5	157	463	387	850	
	Q2	104	30	23	4	180	662	378	1,040	
	Q3	106	34	24+3	2	250	568	226	794	
	Q4	112	33	24	6	160	431	376	807	3,491
1929	Q1	116	42	28	27	140	553	326	879	
	Q2	115	43	28+2	25	177	438	428	866	
	Q3	120	43	34+2	15	190	434	358	792	
	Q4	103	31	21+3	12	175	584	327	911	3,448
1930	Q1	120	40	31	8	175	449	259	708	
	Q2	104	30	24	6	170	438	171	609	
	Q3	118	45	29	9	74	422	139	561	
	Q4	109	38	21		135	434	157	591	2,469
1931	Q1	110	39	20	18	180	353	183	536	
	Q2+3	122	40	32		170	1,083	317	1,400	
	Q4	122	41	30–2	4	146	708	174	982	2,918
1932	Q1	122	39	29+2	4	150	1,023	178	1,201	
	Q2	130	42	34+2	2	120	1,177	1,046	2,223	
	Q3	145	43	39+2	3	117	910	1,767	2,677	
	Q4	150	40	35+3	6	97	1,070	1,867	2,937	9,038
1933	Q1	137	39	36+3	11	220	978	2,286	3,264	
	Q2+3	144	43	38+2	12	646	1,899	3,585	5,484	
	Q4	126	48	35	18	246	845	1,356	2,201	10,949

* Figures after the plus sign represent solved or soluble codes/ciphers, but not meriting on-going decipherment.

@ Texts submitted by the central Cipher Section are in Column (1), those by listening posts in (2), and (1)+(2)=(3)

Foreign Ministry, which tried to insist that all traffic with German military personnel in missions overseas should be sent in Foreign Ministry codes.[38]

CRYPTANALYSIS AND POLICY FORMATION

Apart from the collaborative relationship with the navy and the army on decipherment activity, there is almost no explicit information about co-operative relations with either other German agencies or with any foreign agencies before 1934. What the quarterly reports indicate, however, is that assistance was forthcoming from various parties, usually in the form of solutions to specific codes which could save the military agencies a lot of time, or of actual code materials which may well have been acquired by theft, bribery or espionage. These third parties are usually referred to as 'a friendly quarter', which could mean anything from other sections of the Secret Service (*Abwehr I, III, IV*), to the civilian ministries, or even to the secret services of Hungary, Lithuania, Austria, Spain and Finland, with which significant exchanges of military intelligence were regularly conducted during the 1920s and 1930s.[39]

One general observation about the linkage between the military cryptanalysts and both the Defence and Foreign Ministries that needs to be pointed out is that, for the period of the 1920s and 1930s at least, the archivists had plenty of time to remove virtually all explicit evidence of the 'missing dimension' from their files. Evidence from the quarterly reports themselves shows that duplicate copies were destroyed in 1942–43. Most of the older files of the Army Command had long been removed to Potsdam, where they were almost all destroyed by Allied bombing raids in the closing stages of the war, and it is only in the surviving files of the Naval Command that it is possible to pursue traces of cryptanalytical material. The files of the Naval Intelligence Section, however, contain only a handful of intercepted radio reports and diplomatic cables for the years 1931–34 of very minor significance.[40] These were circulated to the head of the Secret Service and Section I, as well as to the Military Intelligence Section (*T3*) and Naval Intelligence (*AII*), which would have drawn the attention of senior officers to them had they been significant. The individual documents passed on in this way were normally placed in closed envelopes for circulation within the Defence Ministry, which also relayed specific items of military political or military economic significance to the senior officials of the Foreign Ministry. Lots of such plain brown envelopes wound up in the files of the Foreign Ministry, but their original provenance is not identified on paper and could just as readily have been derived from the political intelligence set-up within the Foreign Ministry as from the military agencies.[41]

Scrutinising even the secret archives of the Foreign Ministry for these classes of evidence would be a task of mammoth proportions, and there would be no guarantee of finding explicit evidence that would link foreign policy formation with cryptanalytical evidence or agencies. In any event, given the nature of bureaucratic politics, the external policy priorities of different governmental agencies do not necessarily coincide, even in wartime. But under peacetime conditions, the likelihood is greater of unresolved choices, of shifting priorities even within single agencies, and of competition among and between open and covert intelligence-gathering agencies. Until the end of 1929, following the death of Foreign Minister Stresemann, the evidence suggests that the priorities in German foreign policy were generally determined by the diplomats. In Cabinet, the influence of the army was greatly moderated on specific issues; one good example of this can be found in Stresemann's refusal to go along with the policy of von Schleicher and Gempp in demanding the prosecution of the Social Democratic opposition and of pacifists for 'treasonable' revelation of the covert activities of the military in Russia, Spain and elsewhere.[42] The Foreign Ministry successfully put pressure on the Defence Ministry under General Groener to control covert military agencies through the centralisation of army and navy organisations in the Secret Military Intelligence Service in 1928. But, since the dominant role in this was played by the army, the curbs imposed weighed much more heavily on the navy's operations, as witness the closure of the World Intelligence Service in 1929, which followed complaints from the German Ambassador in Madrid, Hanno von Welczeck.[43]

The organisational changes, however, were used to reinforce the existing army perception of a primary threat from Poland and France, which was increasingly conjoined with the dangers of domestic instability and potential revolution with the onset of the Great Depression which coincided with the death of Stresemann.[44] The Social Democrats, with their political control in Prussia and their revelations about German deals with the Soviet Union, exposed the army's hopes for Soviet strategic relief in the east and also blocked moves to strengthen defences along the borders with Poland. The threat of Polish intervention against Danzig and East Prussia was constantly advanced as a valid reason for maintaining a covert intelligence organisation in the east. The Foreign Ministry conceded in principle, even before Stresemann's death, the need for a National Security Council and for the gathering of military intelligence about Poland. In practice, however, the military's fixation over the Polish threat was viewed as over-exaggerated by the diplomatic mission in Warsaw and by the East European division in the Foreign Ministry. Nevertheless, the existence of a covert organisation meant that the

Defence Ministry could always point to specific reports about Polish provocation and the undoubted evidence of a 'secret war' along the eastern borderlands.[45]

Figure 4 provides an overview of evidence culled from the quarterly reports of the Deciphering Section of the Secret Military Intelligence Service about the distribution of its cryptanalytical efforts. This indicates that the greatest efforts in the form of the allocation of additional resources to 'task forces' were directed towards Eastern Europe. In the eight-year period covered, it was always possible to obtain substantial numbers of decrypts of the diplomatic traffic of the Western Powers without the need to expend extraordinary efforts. Most effort was expended on Polish codes and ciphers with a considerable degree of success until the end of 1930. Soviet support for the German Communist Party and the uncertainty of Soviet support for Germany against Poland, together with the high quality of Soviet codes and ciphers, presented a significant challenge to the German cryptanalysts. Only very limited success was achieved with Soviet diplomatic codes, and the Soviet trade cipher from 1924 to 1927 was retrospectively reconstructed by 1930, while low-grade military, internal security and collective farm wireless networks were extensively resolved until 1932. Low-grade Czech signals were also resolved until the end of 1930, but Czech diplomatic codes remained wholly impregnable throughout the period, although, it has to be conceded, work on these was always subordinated to the demands made by Polish and Soviet codes and ciphers.

The evidence even from German records suggests that the Poles were particularly concerned to alert France to the dangers of German–Soviet collaboration and to maintain the value of Franco-Polish links. This appears to have been the drift of Polish claims in September 1924 of decipherment of German and Soviet signals allegedly exchanged between units of the Red navy and the *Reichsmarine* in autumn manoeuvres in the Baltic. More detailed information about Polish claims was obtained by the German minister in Riga from a foreign (apparently the American) military attaché there, and relayed to General von Seeckt and the Navy Signals Section.[46] The somewhat garbled details sent on from Riga showed that, while it was true that the Poles, with the aid of a reconnaissance aircraft, had monitored brief signals from the old battleship *Braunschweig* and from Soviet vessels, the information was mixed in with the call-signs of Polish and German transmitters, as well as foreign merchant ships at sea. Any claim that the Poles had either deciphered German naval traffic or had established clear evidence of exchanges of signals between Soviet and German warships was dismissed.[47] Of much greater significance for the German navy were post-1919 revelations about the retrieval of codebooks from the cruiser *Magdeburg* in 1914, and they were

FIGURE 4

THE DISTRIBUTION OF CRYPTANALYTICAL EFFORTS
OF GERMAN MILITARY AGENCIES, 1926–1933

Year	1926	1927	1928	1929	1930	1931	1932	1933
Quarter	I II III IV	I II III IV	I II III IV	I II III IV	I II III IV	I II III IV	I II III IV	I II III IV
1. U.S.S.R.	★★★★	★★★★	★★★★	★★★★	★★★★	★☆☆★	★★★☆	☆☆☆☆
2. Poland	★★★★	★★★★	★★★★	★★★★	★★★★	☆☆☆☆	☆☆☆☆	★★★★
3. Lithuania	★							
4. Czecho-slovakia	★ ☆		★★★★	★★★★	★★★★	☆☆☆☆	☆☆☆☆	☆☆☆
5. Rumania	★★ ★		★★★★	★	★★★	★☆☆☆	★★★★	★★★
6. Yugoslavia			★★★	★	★★★★	★★★★	★★★★	★★★
7. Bulgaria					★★☆	☆☆☆		
8. Italy	★★★★	★★★★	★★★★	★★★★	★★★★	★★★★	★★★★	★★★
9. Spain	☆							
10. France	★★★★	★★★★	★★★★	★★★★	★★★★	★★★★	★★★★	★★★★
11. Belgium			★	★★★★	★★★★	★★★★	★★★★	★★★★
12. Netherlands						★★	★★	
13. Britain	★★★★	★★★★	★★★★	★★★★	★★★★	★★★★	★★★★	★★★★
14. U.S.A.	★★★★	★★★★	★★★★	★★★★	★★★★	★★★★	★★★★	★★★★

☆ – unsuccessful efforts at cryptanalysis
★ – successful cryptanalytical activity, but degree of success not necessarily complete
☐ denotes the establishment of a special task force, which often involved taking manpower away from work on other countries' ciphers to reinforce teams working on codes of special policy significance.

an important factor in the selection of the Enigma cipher machine for fleet use in the late 1920s. The mistakes made in the First World War were recognised in a study of 1934 by a member of the Navy Signals Section, Commander Kleikamp.[48] Similar admonitions were circulated to army signals specialists in 1936:

> The view that the monitoring of German radio traffic by foreign armies cannot achieve as much success as German listening-posts is a mistaken one.[49]

Information about German breaches of the Versailles Treaty had been channelled via the Inter-Allied Military Control Commission from many different sources. The German counter-intelligence service claimed knowledge of links between pacifist and left-wing groups in Germany and various Allied representatives inside Germany. After the Commission was formally wound up in April 1927, information continued to be collected by the bureaux of Allied military attachés in Berlin which took a special interest in such questions as the fortification of the eastern borderlands. The German Foreign Ministry was firmly of the view that the Polish government had obtained copies of secret documents on the matter and was keen to stir the matter up with Paris and London.[50] Tension between Germany and Poland increased from 1930 onward, partly as a result of fears of Polish intervention at a time of growing internal unrest in Germany. The fears of the military in Germany appear to have been increased by the increasing frequency of Polish military overflights of German territory from October 1929, which led to repeated protests and proposals by some of the hotter heads in the army for the shooting down of such aircraft.[51] Added to this tension and uncertainty was increasing evidence of a gradual tightening up of Polish diplomatic coded messages and of the inability of the Deciphering Section to resolve many of the ciphers employed by the Polish air force, which was also reorganised, and German intelligence about its order of battle and operating bases confused for long periods between 1930 and 1932.[52]

A major handicap for the German military deciphering agencies was a lack of adequate trained manpower, especially in the early 1920s. If a task force had to be assembled to work on Polish or French codes, manpower had to be diverted from Soviet or Rumanian or Western codes as a direct consequence. The problem eased somewhat in the later 1920s as more trained manpower became available in the listening posts and these took over an increasing proportion of the workload. But the German experience of the technical problems was little different from those of other national agencies in the same period. Where too few signals were sent, statistical methods of breaking codes yielded fewer results. Where cipher clerks made mistakes, the path of the decipherer was distinctly smoothed. Where codebooks and cipher tables could be obtained, the time taken to achieve concurrent resolutions decreased dramatically. The military decipherers appear not to have had the benefit of inside knowledge in dealing with diplomatic codes: unlike the Foreign Ministry, they could not scrutinise the texts of memoranda prepared by senior officials on their interviews with foreign diplomats and then compare these with the texts of encoded intercepts. Sometimes, however, with the less stout codes carrying more routine messages, it was possible to compare newspaper reports and find correlations with official statements or specific names. Many British, US and Rumanian diplomatic messages were resolved by such means, while the structure of the French language was of assistance on many occasions. In the case of telegraphic signals, decipherment was hindered by not having access to sufficient material passing through the national network. Sometimes this could be remedied by obtaining intercepts from friendly foreign powers such as Hungary, but this was usually helpful only in the cases of small states which did not have the resources to produce separate codebooks for different circuits or to change these frequently enough. Radio transmissions became more frequent in the second half of the 1920s, providing large numbers of intercepts of the signals of the Western Powers. But even here things could alter quickly, as for instance the presence of the US Secretary of State at the London Naval Disarmament Conference in 1930 resulted in the switch from wireless to cable circuits between Washington and London.

In the German experience, the country with the laxest code security was unquestionably Italy, which committed all the worst errors in coded communication. At one point, the cipher clerks in Rome got the dates of their cipher tables mixed up and prevented their own diplomats from understanding their messages. Mistakes of this kind, however, provided manna from heaven for third parties, because repetitions of the same messages in different codetables or superencipherments compromised subsequent signals for weeks or months ahead. The Italians were also observed retaining the same superencipherment used on old codes for use with the new, thereby compromising the new codes as well. The Deciphering Section witheringly observed:

> This fact is fresh evidence for the increasingly inadequate capacity the Italians still show in being unable to research critically the security of their own codes against decipherment. A technical enciphering error can always occur, but it is significant that with the Italians the same mistake should keep on being made time and again.
>
> It is also striking that the old codes are still being used as well as the new ones. This is at variance with the past practice of the Italian cipher bureau. It is therefore not out of the question that the Italians, as a result of their recent active involvement in the study of French codes, may well have copied their practice of employing a multiplicity of codes to reduce the numbers of messages in any one code as a means of obstructing foreign unauthorised decipherment![53]

If Italy and Rumania presented the worst cases, the greatest admiration was reserved for the Russians, whose cipher clerks operated with such consistency that on only one occasion in the time period surveyed was a serious encoding error made. This resulted in the decipherment of 117 cables on the Moscow–Berlin circuit for the period March–November 1927. A further error detected on 2 December 1929 appears not to have led to any similar break. The minimum number of messages that had to be despatched in the same code/superencipherment was about 70 per month, but the frequency of changes in Soviet coding arrangements had the effect of the subsequent one-time pad, not introduced into British Foreign Office traffic until 1939. Only the Poles at their best seemed to match the Soviet achievement, and with changes in the international climate after 1931 even those simpler Soviet wireless codes for low-level army and air force traffic that had previously presented no difficulties in the past began to be tightened up and the standard achieved reached that of the Tsarist army at its best in 1916. After 1933, the worsening in German–Soviet relations ensured that the normal intelligence sources that the Germans had come to rely on as a result of mutual collaboration dried up as technical specialists were withdrawn from military and industrial projects. The German military attaché in Moscow, General Köstring, lamented the difficulties of obtaining any information, however harmless, in the Soviet Union. Even when there had been close Soviet–German collaboration, things had been difficult enough, he said. He indicated that he was then trying to make the most use of the consular posts in the Soviet Union, but no sooner had that report been sent than the Soviet authorities closed down all foreign consulates and the sole source of military information, apart from monitoring signals and chatting to other military attachés in Moscow, seems to have been the War Ministry couriers accompanying German diplomatic bags between Berlin and Tokyo after the discovery that these were being opened and resealed by the Soviet internal security secretariat.[54]

Observation of French ciphering arrangements suggested that some codes were initially tried out in areas like the Middle East before being introduced into the principal European circuits. This made it possible to begin work at an early stage on likely ciphers before they were employed in Europe and to cut down the time involved in resolving them or in being able to produce clear texts sooner than if the French had not pursued such a strategy. The French also appeared to seek safety in numbers, but they kept so many codes in use for such a long period of time that any advantage that might have been gained from sheer numbers was wasted. In 1930–31, when the total volume of cipher messages declined drastically, these practices meant that the Germans were able to continue to rely on deciphering substantial numbers of French signals when practically all other countries had introduced new codes and ciphers and simultaneously created a famine in the numbers of clear texts available to German policymakers. The famine was partly created by the general reduction in the numbers of messages despatched, but an upswing was observed in the second quarter of 1931 that was 'assisted by political events which forced diplomats to engage in a more active exchange of views and more detailed reporting'.[55] It would appear that the pressure on the French was particularly intense, for the Deciphering Section noted in March 1931:

> For a time, the extensively active exchange of information placed the French themselves in a very tight spot where they were unable to keep a tight control over their own confidential messages: on 29 March, the French ambassador in Warsaw cabled Paris: 'In view of the problems caused by the decipherment of urgent cipher cables, please send non-urgent telegrams *en clair* that are supposed to be transferred by mail, using the courier between early on Monday

morning and Thursday evening.' The fact that a preference has emerged for the use of plain codes can be linked to this overload.[56]

The accession of the Hitler regime in 1933 seems to have stimulated increased diplomatic traffic in Europe, just as the Japanese intervention in Manchuria had stimulated greater traffic in the autumn of 1931. The Deciphering Section noted in May 1933:

> The considerable political tension in the last few months has resulted, especially in the most recent period, in an extraordinary increase in the cable material being intercepted. This again proves the correctness of the view that in politically interesting times all precautionary measures to safeguard security, such as couriers, relay by air & c., have to be ignored: if the most rapid possible transmission of important information is what matters, then the telegraph is going to come into its own, and in order to save time, even telegrams with the most delicate subject matter will be encoded in the simpler procedures.[57]

Hitler, as is well known, was a man in a hurry, and the tempo in international relations began to speed up from this point in the wake of the Japanese departure from the League, followed a few months later by that of Germany, which also quit the Disarmament Conference for good measure. The steady flow of French and Italian decrypts was matched by an 'extremely successful' interception of British signals, arising mainly from an increased flow of radio transmissions at this period. Similarly, the flow of intercepted US State Department radiograms in both the 'Gray' and 'Green' Codes throughout 1933 was characterised as

> very large, especially in the month of February, because practically the whole of the radio traffic on the Geneva–Washington circuit could be intercepted. As both U.S. observers of the Manchurian conflict and Ambassador Gibson at the Disarmament Conference sent lengthy reports, together with American views on the specific proposals, to the State Department, it was possible to gain a good view of the various committees operating behind the scenes at both conferences.[58]

Since the quarterly reports break off at the end of 1933, the detailed picture that can be built up for the years 1925 to 1933 comes to an end. Only scattered documents and references to decrypts can be culled from the surviving archives between 1934 and 1939. These suggest a regular diet of French, British, Polish, Italian, Japanese and Balkan decrypts reaching the German leadership in a position to live more dangerously thanks to the cryptanalytical windows that had steadily opened up during the Weimar era. The *Forschungsamt* in particular grew at a very rapid rate until it effectively superseded the Decipherment Service of the Armed Forces, which was removed from the direct control of Admiral Canaris by 1938. After 1933, the financial constraints that had been imposed by the Weimar coalition governments were removed and substantial resources were channelled into the expansion of both the military and the civilian deciphering groups.[59] Each of these groups, except the navy, benefited from the employment of personnel who had mainly been trained by the German army and were able to benefit substantially from the mistakes of the past and from a close observation of the mistakes being made by others. When the leaders of other states discussed the policies they proposed with their friends, their ideas and statements were bound to be betrayed by the insecurity of their communication systems, and were open to greatest exploitation by those countries, such as Germany and the Soviet Union, which were prepared to invest heavily in perfecting secure systems of their own and in building up extensive monitoring and deciphering networks. Neither Hitler nor Stalin saw the value or need to consult extensively with allies about their next moves, and could prepare such moves in the knowledge that their own communications systems had achieved a higher degree of security than most of their neighbours and that the autonomous nature of these moves decreased the likelihood of any breach of security through their friends and allies.[60] Hitler appears to have been particularly well-informed through Goering and the *Forschungsamt,* with its substantial manpower of 1,500 in its central offices in Berlin alone in 1942, and with the backing of the Four-Year Plan. At the same time, however, it should be emphasised that German planning in this sphere, as in others such as the war economy in general, was very much geared to the short war calculations of Hitler, in which opponents could be picked off separately one at a time. The proliferation of cryptanalytical agencies that occurred after 1933 was not calculated to cope with a significant number of hostile powers each with greater potential resources than Germany simultaneously, and the inadequacy of the German warfighting system in such conditions as a whole was mirrored in its inability to sustain its earlier cryptological and cryptanalytical advantages.[61]

THE CRYPTOLOGICAL DIMENSION IN THE INTERNATIONAL SYSTEM

Alongside the cross-national comparisons of cryptanalytical and cryptological capabilities that the quarterly reports provide, there is a critical system-wide aspect to be appraised. The historiography of the inter-war period is heavily influenced by an understandable concern for the causes of the Second World War. Those who do not accept 1933 as the most important date of departure often point to a Eurocentric bias in such a

FIGURE 5
ORGANISATION PLAN OF THE GERMAN NAVAL INTELLIGENCE SERVICE, 1935

DESK	DUTIES AND RESPONSIBILITIES	DESK OFFICER
AIII	Section Chief	Captain (R) Arps
	1) Overall control of the Naval Intelligence Service; 2) In charge of the collection of information; central organisation for matters connected with the Signals Service; 3) Co-operation with Army Intelligence Section (T3)	
AIIIa	1) Military, organisational and tactical questions of the Signals Service, including preparation of manuals	Lieut.Cmdr. Mössel (also subordinate to the Signals Desk in the Naval Operations Section (A In)
AIIIa[1]	2) Preparation of the Wartime Signals Service of the Navy	Lieut.Cmdr.v.Mühlendahl
AIIIa[2]	3) Command & Signals Exercises of the C-in-C, Navy	Lieut.Cmdr.(R) Begemann
AIIIa[3]	4) Representative of the Navy in Signals Matters within and outside the Armed Forces	Civilian Assistant Hinz
	5) Questions concerning national and international radio networks, in so far as these affect the military sphere	
	6) Work on our own ciphering systems	
	7) Work on recognition signals (Handbook for Recognition Signals)	
	8) Surveillance of our own radio installations	
	9) Expert of the Signals Service in the Fleet Section	
	10) Co-operation with a) AIVh with respect to fundamental questions of organisation and deployment; b) BB VI so far as these affect the military sphere; c) all budget matters concerning signals	
MNO Berlin	1) Arrangements for the Signals Section, Berlin; 2) cipher traffic of the C-in-C, Navy; 3) cipher traffic for training purposes	Lieut.Cmdr. Mühlendahl
AIIIb	Radio Monitoring & Deciphering Group	
	Head of Radio Monitoring & Deciphering Service	Lieut.Cmdr. Bonatz (also desk officer in the Secret Military Intelligence Section)
AIIIb[1] AIIIb[2] AIIIb[3]	Location of our own and foreign naval forces	Lieut.Cmdr. Garlepp Senior Executive Officer Tranow Senior Executive Officer Franke
AIIIFM	Group for Foreign Navies	Group Chief: Captain Arps
	1) Collection and Evaluation of information about foreign navies; 2) Publication of 'Briefings about Foreign Navies'; 3) supply of compilations about foreign countries to the Army Command; 4) and to the 'Marine Rundschau'; 5) revision of printed pamphlets: Cruiser Handbooks, Foreign Navies, war maps; 6) scrutiny of Weyer's 'Pocketbook of Fleets'; 7) assistance with the possibilities of support for overseas cruisers; winter studies connected with foreign navies; counter-espionage.	
AIIId	Desk expert for France, Spain and Portugal	Commander Boie
AIIIe	Desk expert for Italy and states of the Eastern Mediterranean	Retd.Lieut.Cmdr. Kotthaus
AIIIf	Desk expert for Scandinavia, Poland, Russia, Baltic States	Lieut.Cmdr.(R) Meyer
AIIIg	Desk expert for Great Britain, Holland, South America	Lieut.Cmdr. Gebeschus
AIIIh	Desk expert for the U.S.A., Japan, and smaller Far Eastern states	Lieut.Cmdr. Prause
AIIIn	Assessment of the military requirements for signals equipment/manpower	Lieut.Cmdr. Gadow (AIVh)
AIIIv	Administration	Senior Executive Officer Krüger
AIVh	1) All matters concerning training in the Signals Service, signals exercises of the Fleet and Naval Stations	Lieut. Cmdr. Gadow and Lieut. Cmdr. Nieguth
	2) Military requirements in the development of signals equipment and apparatus of the Navy	
	3) Equipment of ships and shore establishments with signals equipment	
	4) Responsibility for budget matters of the Signals Service	

periodisation and argue for a more holistic or global view requiring 1931 to be seen as the key date. Yet others would point to major discontinuities in the history of the inter-war period arising before either of these dates, with the economic historians laying particular emphasis on the fundamental changes generated in the world economic system after the autumn of 1929. The international system when examined through the prism of cryptanalytical observations seems to identify the onset of discontinuities in the communication systems of the national units as occurring in the course of 1930. The quarterly reports indicate a dramatic decline in the numbers of messages transmitted during 1930 and 1931. The German observers initially explained the decline in the following terms in October 1930:

> The number of clear texts has dropped by comparison with earlier periods. The main reason for this decline is to be ascribed to the greatly restricted exchange of information among Italian, Polish and Rumanian diplomats and finds further expression in the complete gap in the decipherment of some Polish codes. The successor codes involved many weeks of effort before the first results could be submitted. Another factor to be taken into account was the fact that the observations of foreign manoeuvres and the participation of many of the listening-post personnel in their own local training exercises took them temporarily away from their usual duties of interception, with the result that a drop in the amount of material logged was unavoidable.[62]

Such reasons, however, would scarcely account for a 30 per cent decline in the numbers of clear-texts submitted. Confirmation that this was not just a temporary shift, but reflected structural changes in the system as a whole, came in the next quarterly report issued in February 1931:

> The amount of radio messages in the fourth quarter [of 1930] also fell short of the results for earlier periods of time: in the military sphere especially (Army radio stations), a more sparing use of radio communications was observed. Likewise, in diplomatic traffic (both cable and radio) there was a positive prevalence of efforts to try to reduce the length of the messages sent. Without any doubt it has become standard practice to despatch information that is not altogether important by letter, as compared to the past. This restriction in the use of the telegraph is most particularly evident in the cases of Poland, Rumania and Italy. On their own, these moves would have had a disadvantageous impact on concurrent decipherment, but in the last quarter a further blow was felt as a result of the replacement of numerous, previously readable, codes by fresh ciphers, work on which was bound to be time-consuming to some extent. Nevertheless, many of these problems had already been overcome before the end of the year.[63]

Yet, the pattern of increasing difficulty for the German decipherers was one that continued unabated into the first quarter of 1931, when it was noted that

> The partial or complete changes of codes in the foreign ministries of Britain, France, Italy, Yugoslavia and Poland has also continued to have ill-effects in the first quarter: even if such marked progress in all the areas affected by code changes was achieved that it will only be a question of time and of the availability of material before solutions can be attained, a further fall in the numbers of clear-texts will have to be anticipated for a while. Apart from a few exceptions, practically no information of a diplomatic variety is coming from Italian, Polish and British sources which used to be submitted regularly. The bulk of clear texts has been obtained from French sources.[64]

While much of the decline in the numbers of messages could be attributed to financial economies in the wake of the Depression, it could not explain the apparent widespread resort to the introduction of new codes and ciphers. To what this is attributable is uncertain, but it may well suggest that it resulted from system-wide demonstration effects, perhaps reflecting mutual reactions by national cryptanalytical agencies to each other's moves or perhaps reflecting a general uncertainty and apprehension on the part of national decision-makers. The first Polish feelers for a non-aggression pact were evidently put out to the Soviet Union during the autumn of 1930, one of the first steps on the way to the break-up of the Franco-Polish-Japanese alignment against the Soviet Union that had been a central feature of the international system in the 1920s.[65] The French, for their part, were negotiating with the Germans, but evidently gave up in despair and pursued detente with the Russians, provided that the Russians also arrived at a settlement with the Poles. The Japanese army, meanwhile, worried about the effects of Soviet and Chinese rearmament on the military balance in Asia, had come round to the view that Poland's military capabilities as a check to the Soviet Union in Europe were not significant any longer and had intimated a wish to support the idea that 'Germany must have a strong army in order to help keep Russia in check'.[66] While France and Poland decided to accept non-aggression pacts with the Soviet Union, the Japanese army firmly rejected a Soviet proposal to that effect exactly a year after it was proposed by Litvinov at the end of 1931, thus effectively isolating Japan from any European alignment for the first time since 1902.

CONCLUSION

The cryptanalytical evidence appears to confirm a definite shift, therefore, toward a much more fluid international system and the increasingly rapid tempo of change was fully confirmed in the period from the end of 1931 to the end of 1933 covered by the quarterly reports. What we are observing, then, is a basic shift from a peacetime pattern of cryptanalytical activity to a crisis-functioning pattern of a kind that is closer to that of the contemporary era, except that political leaders of the 1930s were far less inhibited by fear of general war than those of the present day whose concern with the nuclear holocaust has brought to the fore the need to rely more heavily on communications intelligence to underpin strategies of damage limitation and conflict avoidance. The German quarterly reports provide clear hints of the advantages that a bold and dynamic risk-taking leadership could derive from superior cryptological capabilities, but they do not as such provide any clear answers to questions about why their opponents, having evidently been ahead of the Germans in deciphering the Soviet diplomatic codes up to 1927, fell so badly behind them in both cryptographic and cryptanalytical skills in the 1930s. No one, for example, has yet answered the question put forward by the late Donald McLachlan in 1968, when he argued that 'it will be a crucial task for the naval historian of the Thirties to find out precisely why, and with what degree of care and thought, the [*British*] Naval Staff of those days rejected a similar change [*from hand-constructed ciphers to machines*] for the Fleet'.[67] The fact that GC&CS apparently failed to make much headway with resolving German diplomatic codes of the 1930s and had far less to show than the Poles or the French by 1939 toward an understanding of the 'Enigma' system (the commercial version of which the US military attaché in Berlin had bought for a few dollars in the 1920s) suggests a rather lamentable degree of commitment to that acme of strategy, winning without resort to war, for which the Ultra achievement in the course of a Pyrrhic victory is but a poor substitute.

NOTES

1. *Documents on German Foreign Policy, 1918–1945*, Series D, Vol.XII, Nos.639 and 645.
2. Hewel memorandum of 30 May 1943 from the Berghof to Foreign Minister von Ribbentrop about the contact man of *Abwehr I Luft/Ost*, Dr Ivar Lissner, refers to the 'well-known antipathy of the Führer towards self-styled secret agents'. *Auswärtiges Amt: Politisches Archiv, Bonn: Pol I M g.Rs: 'Russland, Lissner', Bd.1, (1942–1944)*. Lissner, like another *Abwehr* contact in Sweden, Dr Edgar Claus, who was expelled by the Swedes in 1943, was accused of having Jewish connections and seems to have been the victim of systematic Gestapo efforts to discredit Admiral Canaris and the *Abwehr*.
3. See the memorandum by De Witt C. Poole to James W. Riddleberger, 'The Nazi Experience in its Foreign Political Aspect', in National Archives, Washington DC, Record Group 59, State Decimal File, 840.00116 E.W./12.745. The main source was the *Forschungsamt* decrypts and telephone taps supplied to Hitler by Goering: see David Kahn, *The Codebreakers* (London: Sphere Books, 1973), Chapter 12, and David Irving, *Breach of Security* (London: Kimber, 1968).

4. See Gessler circular *Reichswehrminister (Heer) Nr.447/24 geh. Tl.III* of 8 Oct. 1924 and Wetzell circular *Der Chef des Truppenamtes Nr.30/26 geh.Kdos.TA.II* of 1 April 1926 in *Bundesarchiv/Militärarchiv* RH12-1/v.40, pp.137 and 237-8, and Sir J. Wheeler-Bennett, *The Nemesis of Power* (London: Macmillan, 1953), p.184.
5. For an elucidation of the confused and confusing terminology over SIGINT, see F.H. Hinsley, *British Intelligence in the Second World War* (London: HMSO, 1979), Vol.I, p.21n; and C.M. Andrew & D. Dilks (eds.), *The Missing Dimension* (London: Macmillan, 1984).
6. Quoted in Immanuel Wallerstein, *The Modern World-System* (New York: Academic Press, 1974), p.8.
7. See *Reichswehrministerium: Abwehr-Abteilung: Chiffrierstelle: 'Entzifferungsberichte', (1925-1933)*.
8. See, for example, Patrick Beesly, *Room 40* (London: Hamish Hamilton, 1982); and David Kahn, 'Codebreaking in World Wars I and II', in Andrew and Dilks, op. cit., Chapter 7.
9. Hinsley, op. cit., Chapter 1, which essentially operates within the brief of the official histories of the Second World War laid down soon after 1945. See, however, the forthcoming study on surprise and deception in British foreign policy by Professor D.C. Watt.
10. K.N. Waltz, *Theory of International Politics* (Reading, MA: Addison-Wesley, 1979), esp. Chapter 2.
11. G. Barraclough, *An Introduction to Contemporary History* (Harmondsworth: Penguin Books, 1983), Chapter 2; K.W. Deutsch, *The Nerves of Government* (New York: Free Press, 1966), Chapters 2 and 3.
12. Cf. D. Landes, *The Unbound Prometheus* (London: Cambridge University Press, 1970), pp.423-30.
13. Zenker memorandum *Chef Admiralstab Nr.798 B* of 7 March 1919 to the Head of the Navy delegation at the Peace Conference in Spa, *Reichswehrministerium: Marineleitung: Marine-Friko: Akte 91: 'Neuregelung des Welt-Nachrichten-Verkehrs,' (1919)*. German cables had been cut by the British early in the First World War, which had increased some German use of wireless, but had also made the interception of German diplomatic telegrams more difficult. The German side sought to retaliate against British cables with small success using U-boats. The proposal was again raised early in the Second World War, but rejected. Warnings were also issued in 1940 about the British Secret Service being supplied with intercepted German and Italian cables in Spain by the British-owned Italcable network and by Sosthenes Behn of ITT. See Beesly, op. cit., p.2; *OKW Abwehrabteilung III Nr.95071/40/6781g Abw III F 6* of 19 Oct. 1940 in *O.K.W.: Ausland III: 'Etappenwesen, Besonderes', Bd.6, (1940-1941)*, p.278.
14. See A. Sampson, *The Sovereign State of ITT* (New York: Stein & Day, 1973).
15. The various foreign missions in Addis Ababa apparently used their transmitters as a more reliable means of communication with each other in the internal upheavals that attended the conflict. The German Foreign Ministry's code and cipher expert, Curt Selchow, a former army signals officer in the First World War, appears to have established a closer working relationship with the secret service only from the summer of 1936. See the memorandum by Commander Michels of 13 June 1936 in *Reichskriegsministerium: Abteilung Abwehr (V): Akte III-1: 'Etappenwesen, Allgemeines', Bd.5, 1935-1937*.
16. Code H was issued to all German merchant vessels overseas between November 1934 and January 1935, and was intended for use between warships and merchantmen at sea. It was strictly forbidden to use this code for superencipherment of messages with an operational content as it was insufficiently secure. German cruisers on training missions overseas were equipped with 800-watt transmitters and were controlled from a 20-kW transmitter at Friedrichsort near Kiel in peacetime, and later in wartime from the public transmitter at Norddeich. See the background paper 'Funkverkehr mit Auslandskreuzern' used at a briefing of Admiral Raeder on 1 November 1934 in *O.K.M.: 1.Skl.IIa: Akte 2-1: 'Handelskrieg,' Bd.1, (1934-1936)*.

Very few messages were sent in Enigma ciphers by German warships at sea before 1937. Enigma-based signals on any scale to come to the attention of GC and CS in Britain from 1936 were three-rotor machines supplied to the Spanish and Italians during the Spanish Civil War. See Hinsley, op. cit., Vol.I, p.488. German records indicate that four A-type and five K-type cipher machines were in use by the Spaniards and a further nine by the Italians, six of which remained unaccounted for. The traceable Italian machines were returned to the Germans in the autumn of 1939. Discussions had already begun between *Abwehr I M* and the Italian *S.I.S.* at the time of the Munich Crisis about secure communications for the exchange of secret intelligence, and modified versions of the Enigma machines used in Spain were brought back into service in 1939–40. German navy machines were later supplied to the Italian navy to prevent a loss of security after Italian submarines were despatched to the west coast of France for operations in the Atlantic. See *O.K.M.: M Att: 'Italien, Nachrichtenaustausch und Zusammenarbeit', Bd.1, (1938–1940)*.
17. See Michels (*Abwehr Ii*) minute of 13 June 1936 on a consultation with army Captain Rasehorn (*Abwehr Ii*); Commander Krüger (*Abwehr IVb*) minute of 20 Jan. 1937; *OKM/3.Skl.N 3971/39 g.Kdos* of 19 July 1939; *OKW/WFA/Stb WNV/NV III 350/40 g.Kdos* of 2 March 1940 to Selchow. *O.K.W.: Abwehr V: 'Etappenwesen, Allgemeines', Bd.5; O.K.M.: 1.Skl.Ic: 'Marinepolitische Angelegenheiten,' Bd.4; Auswärtiges Amt: Pol I M g.Rs: 'Abwehr, Allgemein Einbau', Bd.1, (1940–1942)*.
18. Captain Steffan (Stockholm) *B.Nr.290/36 GKdos* of 9 April 1936 to Commander v.d.Forst in *O.K.M.: M–IV: 'Attaché – und Auslandsangelegenheiten', Bd.1, (1934–1936)*, pp.385–7. Hagelin appears to have sold a number of BC38 models to the German army after the defeat of France and knowledge of Hagelin's equipment proved useful in 1943, as a result of the sale of his machines to the United States, in achieving some success with some US army ciphers using this equipment.
19. *O.K.M.: 1.Skl.: KTB, Teil B, Heft VI: 'Marinenachrichtendienst, B-Dienst,' (1943)*.
20. In 1933/34, the military security section (*Abwehr III*) reported two members of an army signals section on manoeuvres leaving their cipher machine on the ground and their vehicle unattended for less than half an hour and returning to find it gone. Under the 1914 secrecy laws they could only be sentenced to a short gaol sentence and confinement to barracks for a month. But soon after Hitler came to power the treason laws were rewritten and the death penalty was introduced for offences that had not previously carried it. A naval radio operator who was caught photographing cipher material on board his ship after July 1934 was executed on 11 July 1935. See *Abw.III Nr.551/9.34g* of 15 Oct. 1934 in *Reichskriegsministerium: Abwehr-Abteilung IIIa: 'Handakte IIIa', Bd.III (1935–1936)*. The Polish Military Intelligence Service was certainly regarded as the main perpetrator of break-ins into military buildings and of losses of secret materials, followed by the French and Czechs, especially before 1934. Large quantities of Defence Ministry documents were known to have been leaked to the celebrated Polish agent, Colonel Jerzy Sosnowski, who was apprehended in the autumn of 1933 and whose exchange for German agents in Polish gaols was agreed to by Hitler in early April 1936. The losses of both cipher tables and machines can be verified, but no clear evidence can be found linking these specific losses to any single foreign power, which could just as easily have been the Soviet Union as Poland, though there is no reason for doubting the claims of General Bertrand and Colonel Paillole. See Hinsley, op. cit. Vol.I, p.488 and Stengers in Andrew and Dilks, op. cit., pp.126–37.
21. Report of the visit of Captain Canaris to Budapest, 4–7 April 1935; Johannesson circular *Abw. 4363/6.35 IIIa g.* of 4 July 1935; Schwantes circular *Abwehr-Abteilung Nr.2134/28g Abw.Abt.II* of 26 Nov. 1928; Götting minute *RWM/W Id 188/30g* of 10 April 1930 to General Staff.
22. Rumours about clandestine German military activities in the Soviet Union had been circulated at least since 1925, particularly in the left-wing press and had been kept suppressed by the use of the treason laws of 1914. But it was not until the claims were taken up in the *Manchester Guardian* of 3 Dec. 1926 that the dam broke and the German press produced a surfeit of scandals. See *Auswärtiges Amt: Büro RM: 'Militärwesen', Bd.1, (1920–1929)*.

23. Von Schleicher *RWM/W Nr.148/28 Gkds* of 14 March 1928 to Naval Command; submission by Captain Loewenfeld to Rear-Admiral Pfeiffer, *zu AII 310/28 Gkds* of 20 March 1928. *R.W.M.: Marineleitung: AI-III: 'Verschiedenes', Bd.1, (1923–1929).*
24. See Figure 1. De Haas memorandum *IIIE 2700* of 25 June 1929 in *Auswärtiges Amt: Büro RM: 'Militärwesen', Bd.1, (1920–1929).*
25. See *Reichswehrministerium: Marineleitung: A I u, 'U-Bootsabwehr und Horchwesen', (1929).* Various tests of echo-sounding equipment were carried out in collaboration with the Spanish and Swedish navies and Admiral Spindler, the leading submariner in the Weimar navy, was confident that German echo-sounding was superior to that of other countries. Efforts were made to collect information about the 'Asdic' equipment spotted on British warships and attempts were made to inspect this more closely both officially and covertly by electronics specialists in 1936–37.
26. Major-General Gempp produced his history, based on the war diary of the VIIth Army Corps under the title *Geheimer Nachrichtendienst und Spionageabwehr des Heeres*, in 1928.
27. The idea of a properly centralised intelligence service, embracing political and economic intelligence, had been put forward already in 1930 by the former Chief of the Naval Command, Admiral Behncke, to the Reich Chancellor. See the memorandum by Adolf von Bülow of 30 April 1935 to Foreign Minister von Neurath in *Auswärtiges Amt: Büro RM, 'Sammlung von Agenten-Berichten', (1922–1935).*
28. *Chiffrierstelle Nr.213/33 g.Kdos* of 17 Nov. 1933 noted that the loss of six deciphering staff had resulted in a temporary build-up of data, but that that backlog had rapidly been cleared by 'loyal' staff and by nine new cryptanalysts drafted in from the army listening posts. It stimulated further recruitment and training programmes and the replacements handling Italian traffic actually spotted and logged 20 Italian communication circuits compared to the 12 identified by their predecessors. It is not known if the alleged 'playboy' Hans-Thilo Schmidt, identified as the main provider of documents to the French about the Enigma system ('Asché') was among the latter in Group South of the *Chiffrierstelle*. Source as Note 7 above, and see Hinsley, op. cit., Vol.I, p.488.

The navy's Italian cryptanalyst, too, had been pensioned off in 1930, apparently suffering from a 'brain disease' without ever having made a single successful decrypt. See Junkermann memorandum *TMJ B.Nr. G.P. 984 N* of 26 June 1930 in: *Reichswehrministerium: Marineleitung: M I: 'Verschiedenes,' Heft 2, (1929–1931).*
29. *Chiffrierstelle Nr.60/31 g.Kdos* of 21 Oct. 1931: source as Note 7.
30. See *Luftarchiv: Akte In 1, 433: In 1, V 'Grundlegende L-Verfügungen', (1930–1933), BA/MA, RH12-1/v.115; R.W.M.: Marineleitung: A IIIa-1: 'Verschiedenes', Bd.1, (1933–34).*
31. Götting *W Id 188/30g* of 10 April 1930 in *R.K.M.: W Abt/Inland: Geheim Akten 47. n.14: 'Rundfunk, Kurzwellensender, Lauschmikrophonen, usw.', (1928–1938).*
32. The original signed copy is to be found in the archives of the Military Security Group (*Abwehr III*), but the relevant file unfortunately does not indicate what specifically occasioned the need for the agreement in the first place. But, needless to say, it was not an agreement by which the Gestapo or Hitler felt bound. See *O.K.W.: Amt Ausland/Abwehr: Abwehr-Abteilung III: 'Handakte IIIa', (1933–1935).*
33. *RWM Nr.43/34 g.Kdos TA/T.2 III/In 7 IV/Abw II* of 22 March 1934 in *R.W.M.: Marineleitung: AIIIa-1: 'Verschiedenes,' Bd.1, (1933–34).*
34. See *R.W.M.: Chef der Heeresleitung: 'Aussenpolitik', (1934–5); R.K.M.: Marineleitung: A Ia I: 'Allgemeines', Bd.3, (1933–1940).*
35. See Note 28 above.
36. Cf. Ernst Ritter (ed.), *Reichskommissar für Überwachung der öffentlichen Ordnung und Nachrichtenstelle im Reichsministerium des Innern* (Munich, 1979). The quarterly reports indicate approaches from the Police Presidium in Berlin for help with the decipherment of book-based Soviet and Comintern codes intercepted in the course of anti-Communist activities. Coded radio signals supplied by the Comintern had been identified by the political police as early as 1921 transmitted from Nauen to Moscow as part of the diplomatic privilege enjoyed by the Soviet Trade Mission in Berlin. See Weismann *Tgb.Nr.26629/21g* of 27 April 1921 to Cabinet ministers, including the

defence minister in *Auswärtiges Amt; Geheim Akten: Abteilung IV Russland: Akte Po.19: 'Kommunismus, Sozialismus, usw. in Russland', Bd.1, (1920–1)*. *Chiffrierstelle Nr.82/30 g. Kdos* of 24 Oct. 1930 argued that the plain text of some Comintern signals at that date were in a language like Esperanto. *Chiffrierstelle Nr.25/31 g. Kdos* of 19 May 1931 stated:

> A third party made available information about a Comintern code (Wilhelm Pieck, Berlin), which coincided with the outcome of earlier investigation by the Deciphering Section, but the information provided was too limited for it to be possible to resolve the code.

37. This can be illustrated in the collaboration between the navy wireless station on Borkum and the cruiser *'Köln'* in the monitoring of Royal Navy signals during rescue operations in the Channel involving the submarine M-2 in 1932.
38. In 1940, for example, Counsellor Fenner suggested to the navy that the Foreign Ministry's minor code in use with the smaller missions in Latin America was insufficiently secure for operational messages, and the navy resisted all pressure from the Foreign Ministry to have naval attachés abroad give up use of navy ciphers. See Ribbentrop letter *Pol I M 369/42 g.Rs* of 23 Feb. 1942 and Keitel reply *Chef OKW Nr.0012/42 g.Kdos* of 14 March 1942 in *Auswärtiges Amt: Botschafter Ritter: 'O.K.M.', Bd.2, (1942–1944)*.
39. There are specific references to the acquisition of Russian, Italian and Balkan code materials in the quarterly reports.
40. For example, a Polish army radio message from Warsaw to Paris in 1931, a Soviet diplomatic cable from Geneva to Moscow in 1933, and a Yugoslav cable from Belgrade to Berlin of Dec. 1934.
41. A political intelligence service functioned within the East European division of the German Foreign Ministry using special ciphers prepared by Counsellor Selchow. Baron von Maltzahn also had a string of informants, including foreign correspondents, who kept him apprised of developments as far afield as China, rather as Sir Robert Vansittart used such individuals as Group-Captain Christie. There were a number of such people connected with the Air Ministry who established connections with German figures in the 1920s and 1930s: the Baltic Baron de Ropp, who developed contacts with Rosenberg in the 1930s, and the Marquis of Clydesdale, the unwitting host of the Führer's deputy in 1941.
42. See Köpke memorandum of 18 December 1926 about the case of Karl Mertens in *Auswärtiges Amt: Geheim Akten: Abteilung II F-M: 'Strafverfahren wegen Landesverrat', Bd.1, (1924–1932)*.
43. Welczeck letter of 1 March 1929 to State-Secretary von Schubert in: ibid., *Abteilung II F-Luft: 'Verhandlung über die Entsendung von Luftattachés', Bd.1, (1927–1934)*; von Bredow *M.A. Nr.183/29 Abw. Abt. g. Kdos* of 19 July 1929 in: *R.W.M.: Marineleitung: M I: 'Verschiedenes', Bd.1, (1922–1929)*.
44. See *T2 Nr.1086/30 Pl.IIIa* of 11 Nov. 1930 which outlined a scenario involving a threat to East Prussia combined with internal upheaval: source as Note 30 above.
45. See Zechlin memorandum *e.o. IV Po 3471* of 18 April 1928 on a conversation with Defence Minister Groener in: *Auswärtiges Amt: Geheim Akten: Abteilung IV Polen: Akte Po.10, Nr.1: 'Deutsche Militär-Attaché in Polen', (1928–1935)*. Suspected Polish agents had been arrested as early as January 1920 and defence minister Gessler had cried wolf about a Polish seizure of Marienwerden and Allenstein in East Prussia at least since May 1920. The loss of Upper Silesia to Poland in 1924 had been a very bitter reverse for Germany and subsequently complaints were made about the activities of Captain Zychon of Polish military counter-intelligence against the *Volksbund* organisation there, and later at Danzig. Ibid., *Akte Po.15: 'Agenten-und Spionagewesen-Fall Zychon', (1928–1934)*.

In the autumn of 1930, a series of questions on foreign policy issues originating with the Secret Service were passed on to the Foreign Ministry by defence minister Groener. Among these was the question: has Poland undertaken any military steps (armaments, closer liaison with France) as a result of recent events in Germany? Minister Rauscher in Warsaw responded in a letter of 25 October 1930 to the effect that all the signs were that the Polish government was more concerned about a Soviet threat than with intervention in Germany. Ibid., *Abteilung II F-M: 'Militärische Nachrichten', Bd.1, (1928–1932).*

46. Schubert letter *zu IV Ru 7760g* of 27 December 1924 to General von Seeckt in ibid., *Abteilung IV Russland: Akte Po.14: 'Marineangelegenheiten in Russland', Bd.1, (1924–26)*
47. Pfeiffer letter *RWM/ML/AIII G.Stbs. 39/25* of 15 May 1925 to the Foreign Ministry: ibid.
48. See Beesly, op.cit., Chapter 3, p.29. One of the errors repeated by the German navy in the Second World War was the failure to make cipher changes immediately on learning of the loss of warships carrying cipher tables. The concealment of German losses by the Royal Navy in 1941 was particularly important in making the early breaks in 'Enigma' traffic. Many of the German navy's machine ciphers, however, were never broken. On the other hand, the German navy's small cryptanalytical unit was managing to read a very high percentage of British naval ciphers especially in the period 1939–42, having collaborated closely with the Italians on British and French cipher traffic from 1934 onwards. They were helped, too, by the capture of cipher tables, operational logs and D/F data from British warships such as HM Submarine *Seal* and the liner *Automedon* in 1940, and MGB 235 in 1942. The *Automedon* was caught off Singapore by the raider *Atlantis* with the complete military mail for the Far East Command, including new ciphers for merchant shipping, naval staffs and warships, attachés, and the Secret Intelligence Service posts in Singapore, Shanghai and Tokyo. See the author's *The Price of Admiralty* (Ripe: Saltire Press, 1984), Vol.2, pp.326–7.
49. Von Fritsch circular *ObdH/AHA/In 7 Ic Nr.1910/36g* of 30 July 1936 in *R.K.M.: W.A./Inland: Geheim Akten 47.n.14: 'Rundfunk, Kurzwellensender, Lauschmikrophonen, usw.,' (1928–1938)*.
50. See Forster memorandum *e.o. II F 2301 g.g.* of 30 June 1928 in *Auswärtiges Amt: Geheim Akten: Abteilung II F-M: 'Militärpolitik', Bd.1, (1927–1932).* A British journalist informed Ambassador Sthamer in London in February 1929 that the Foreign Secretary, Sir Austen Chamberlain, was anxious to play down reports constantly coming from Berlin about secret German military preparations in breach of the Versailles Treaty and secret links with the Soviet Union. The British Embassy in Berlin was allegedly not passing on many of these reports to London simply in order to prevent information being compiled in replies to questions in Parliament.

The French, as it turned out, had managed to purchase details of the territorial defence organisation in Saxony from one of its German employees in July 1929 for 10,000 francs. Much detailed information from the German Defence Ministry undoubtedly also reached the Polish General Staff at this period (1925–1933) from Colonel Sosnowski, who also developed good contacts within the expanding Nazi Party. The Defence Ministry was aware of some kind of significant leak at this period, while the Poles were worried both by the centrality of Poland in German operational planning and by the growth in the political influence of the right-wing parties after 1929. See Jonathan Haslam, *Soviet Foreign Policy, 1930–1933* (London: Macmillan, 1983), Chapter 6.
51. *Luftarchiv: In 1.310: Akte A XI,1: 'Richtlinien für die Behandlung von militärischen Grenzverletzungen, Allgemeines', (1925–1931); A XX, 2: 'Grenzverletzungen durch polnische Flugzeuge im Jahre 1930–1933'. BA/MA, RH12-1, v.13 and v.103.*
52. *Chiffrierstelle Nr.60/31 g.Kdos* of 21 October 1931, *Nr.6/32 g.Kdos* of 16 January 1932, *Nr.36/32 g.Kdos* of 22 April 1932, *Nr.68/32 g.Kdos* of 29 July 1932 (which confirmed that 'in spite of tremendous efforts, it has not been possible to record any success with the code employed by Air Force radio stations'), *Nr. 106/32 g.Kdos* of 25 October 1932. Breaks began to be made in the final quarter of 1932 and it was finally resolved in early 1933: *Chiffrierstelle Nr.12/33 g.Kdos* of 23 January 1933 and *Nr.61/33 g.Kdos* of 11 May 1933. Source as Note 7 above.
53. *Chiffrierstelle Nr.21/34 g.Kdos* of 25 January 1934: ibid.
54. Köstring *B.Nr.6/36, Beilage I* of 24 February 1936 in *Auswärtiges Amt: Geheim Akten: Abteilung IIF-M: 'Militär-Attaché Moskau (auch Kowno)', Bd.5, (1935–6).* Keitel

circular *Der RKM und ObdW Nr.392/37 g. Kdos Ausl.IIa* of 7 October 1937 in *Ȯ.K.M.: M IV: 'Attaché–und Auslandsangelegenheiten', Bd.3, (1937–8),* p.11. Keitel subsequently informed Counsellor Schliep of the Foreign Ministry that he was prepared to offer the Soviet Union two consular posts in Germany if Germany could retain consular posts in the USSR.
55. *Chiffrierstelle Nr.60/31 g. Kdos* of 21 October 1931: source as Note 7 above.
56. *Chiffrierstelle Nr.25/31 g. Kdos* of 19 May 1931: ibid.
57. *Chiffrierstelle Nr.61/33 g. Kdos* of 11 May 1933: ibid.
58. Ibid.
59. Figure 5 shows how small the German navy's deciphering unit *(AIIIb)* still was in 1935. It also illustrates how closely integrated it was with the signals *(AIIIa)* and technical signals *(AIV)* desks, intelligence *(AIIIFM* and *Abw.II Chi),* and operations *(AI* and *MNO).* A permanent night watch was mounted within the Defence Ministry to liaise with the *B-Dienst* from August 1934 onward as part of the mobilisation planning of the naval staff in the event of an international crisis.
60. The insecurity of Italian codes and ciphers was consistently observed by various German agencies and only limited efforts made to improve that situation. Hitler appears to have identified Italian lack of security as a major source of leakage up to 1941 and preferred to speak directly to Mussolini when passing on important information. Hitler appears to have had a higher regard for the maintenance of discretion by the Japanese, mainly, it would appear, because the German Foreign Ministry at least was unable to break the main embassy code used by the Japanese Foreign Ministry. Although it was known that the Western Powers had made inroads into Japanese diplomatic codes, Hitler persisted in transmitting detailed information about his operational plans (especially in the East, from 3 June 1941 onward to the Japanese Ambassador, General Oshima), thereby providing the Allies with first-rate strategic intelligence during the Second World War. See National Archives, Washington D.C., Record Group 457, Records of the National Security Agency, SRDG & SRDJ: Japanese/German Diplomats.
61. The German navy's deciphering service, admittedly one of the smaller ones, was forced to contemplate the possibility of abandoning coverage of many of the enemy systems through a lack of sufficient skilled manpower in the summer of 1942. Competition among the various different cryptanalytical agencies was intense, but the basic fact remained that the organisation could not cope with the demands placed on it by the entry of both the Soviet Union and the United States into the war at a time when it was becoming increasingly difficult to resolve the rapidly improving British coding procedures. See the memorandum *O.K.M. 856/42 Chefs.* of June 1942 to Grand-Admiral Raeder on the organisation and manpower levels of the Navy's central deciphering agency *(B-Leitstelle)* in *O.K.M.: 1.Skl.: 'KTB, Teil B VI: Marinenachrichtendienst, B-Dienst', (1942).*
62. *Chiffrierstelle Nr.82/30 g. Kdos* of 24 October 1930: source as Note 7 above.
63. *Chiffrierstelle Nr.7/31 g. Kdos* of 7 February 1931: ibid.
64. *Chiffrierstelle Nr.60/31 g. Kdos* of 21 October 1931: ibid.
65. Haslam, op.cit., p.68 and fn.54. An intercepted telegram from the Finnish Foreign Minister to their Minister in Germany stated that the Poles did not intend to renew the military convention with France and had put out feelers for a non-aggression pact with the USSR. State-Secretary von Bülow cabled Ambassador Hoesch in Paris on 16 January 1931 asking him to consult with the Finnish Minister there to find out if confirmation could be obtained, especially in view of the fact that the Finns and Poles were on intimate terms and exchanged military intelligence about the Soviet Union on a regular basis. *Auswärtiges Amt: Geheim Akten: Abteilung IV Polen: Akte Po.3: 'Politische Beziehungen Polens zu Frankreich', (1920–1933).* There was a regular exchange of information and views between the German army's Intelligence Section *(T3)* and the East European desk in the Foreign Ministry at this time, but the evidence from the quarterly reports is that the Deciphering Section was not actively deciphering Finnish diplomatic cables to Berlin. But it is highly likely that such work was being undertaken by the Foreign Ministry cipher bureau under Counsellor Selchow.

66. Erdmannsdorff (German chargé in Tokyo) Report J.No.1657 in *Auswärtiges Amt: Geheim Akten: Abteilung IV Ostasien: Akte Po.13: 'Militärische Angelegenheiten Japans'*, Bd.2, *(1927–1932)*. Similar views about the limited warfighting capabilities of the Polish armed forces were expressed to the Germans by Finnish and Red Army officers. The Poles themselves felt that the Germans were actually relatively stronger in 1930 than they had been in July 1914 and regarded themselves as much better informed about the real strength of the German armed forces than the French were.
67. D.McLachlan, *Room 39* (London: Weidenfeld & Nicolson, 1968), p.77.

The Government Code and Cypher School Between the Wars

A. G. DENNISTON

In paragraph 10 of 'Post-War Intelligence', a memorandum by Group-Captain Jones,[1] occurs the remark in large type:

> It would indeed be a tragic and retrograde step for intelligence as a whole, and therefore – this is not putting it too high – for the future of the country, if GC and CS were to sink back into its pre-war position.

I think I am right in taking these words *not* as a general scathing criticism of the pre-war activities of GC and CS but as a warm tribute to the efficiency of the wartime development in GC and CS of its new function of 'Intelligence' at the source, a tribute with which, I am sure, none of the service departments will quarrel.

But in justice to the late Admiral[2] and to the members of the peace organisation of GC and CS who, for 20 years fulfilled their allotted task and reached 1939 with a solid foundation on which to build, I propose to state quite briefly for the information of those now about to build a new GC and CS:

> A The origin and purpose of the 1919 GC and CS;
> B Its establishment under Treasury control;
> C Its development.

Files and records sent to safety in 1940 are not available to me, therefore I write from memory and cannot claim complete accuracy in dates and numbers. But the main facts can be substantiated by the evidence of others who took part during those 20 years.

A [THE ORIGIN AND PURPOSE OF THE 1919 GC AND CS]

1. During the 1914–18 war cryptography was practised in two sections:
   (a) *40 OB*,[3] principally German naval, latterly a certain amount of diplomatic enemy and neutral, only using material obtained by interception of W/T by stations under Admiralty control, and
   (b) *MI 1B*, principally German military and (currently) some neutral and later even Allied diplomatic, the raw material for the latter

being obtained from Cable Censorship under War Office control. Only from 1917 was there any exchange between (a) and (b) and then principally of results.
2. Early in 1919 the Cabinet decided that the results obtained by these two sections justified the formation of a permanent section to keep alive the study of this work which had such an important effect on the prosecution of the war, both naval and military.
3. Admiral Sinclair (then DNI)[4] was given the task of forming a section from the remnants of 40 OB and MI 1B, to be established under the civil administration in the Admiralty. Negotiations between Admiralty, War Office and Treasury continued through spring and summer of 1919 and in November or December the new organisation was set up in Watergate House (staff details under B).
4. The present [1944] Ambassador to Peru (Courtenay Forbes), then in the Communications Department of the Foreign Office, invented the title Government Code and Cypher School.
5. The public function was 'to advise as to the security of codes and cyphers used by all Government departments and to assist in their provision'.
6. The secret directive was 'to study the methods of cypher communications used by foreign powers'.
7. Nothing in this constitution indicated how raw material was to be obtained. But DNI, being in charge, was able to retain a small party, both in the Admiralty and War Office, drawn from their rapidly diminishing war time intercepting stations. Pressure from DNI and others procured the inclusion in the New Official Secrets Act[5] of a clause instructing all cable companies operating in UK to hand over for scrutiny copies of all cable traffic passing over their systems within 10 days of despatch or receipt.
8. Nothing in the constitution indicated that it was desirable that successful results of the study should be made available to government departments who might be interested, though in actual practice there was a circulation of 'unprocessed' decodes from the day of our birth, which has continued until today without interruption.
9. In 1921 the Geddes[5] axe fell on us and we moved to Queen's Gate where we were more comfortable but rather remote from other departments. But we were nearer Melbury Road,[7] and when the Admiral took over in 1923 he, as our founder, at once took steps to bring the two organisations[8] into closer touch; this process culminated in 1925, when both moved to the third and fourth floors of Broadway Buildings.[9]
10. About 1922 after two or three years' work and circulation in which results showed that *there was no service traffic ever worth circulating*,

the late Lord Curzon, then Foreign Secretary, claimed that GC and CS was doing work solely for the Foreign Office and should therefore be transferred from the Admiralty to the Chief Clerk's Department of the Foreign Office for administrative purposes. The Admiralty, at that time in process of cutting down, willingly assented and thenceforward GC and CS estimates appeared in the Foreign Office vote.
11. It must be remembered that beyond a salary and accommodation vote GC and CS had no financial status; it became in fact an adopted child of the Foreign Office with no family rights, and the poor relation of the SIS, whose peacetime activities left little cash to spare.

B [ESTABLISHMENT OF GC AND CS UNDER TREASURY CONTROL]

1. GC and CS began with a sanctioned establishment of 25 pensionable officers as follows:
    1 head
    6 senior assistants
    18 junior assistants

   A clerical staff (unpensionable) was also sanctioned, amounting to approximately:
    6 typists
    12 clerks (for code construction)
    10 traffic sorters and slipreaders

2. The pay of the senior staff was based on that of the Administrative Class in the Civil Service, that is:
    senior assistants = principals
    junior assistants = assistant principals

   In due course members of our staff were considered to be eligible for membership of the Association of First Division Civil Servants as are the senior staff in the museums, but there has never been any question of precise equality of pay.

3. On the other hand, when we had to recruit new staff through the Civil Service Commission our candidates did not have to sit for the Administrative Class examination but were selected on interview and record by the Committee of the Commission in which GC and CS was represented.

4. The original selection in 1919 for all classes was made from volunteers who had served in the Admiralty or War Office. Where the needs of the work required special qualifications such as Japanese (Mr Hobart-Hampden) [10] or a highly experienced but already elderly man (Mr Fetterlein) [11] who could not be made pensionable, they were granted equal pay with the others and blocked posts in the establishment. The Chief Clerk had difficulty more than once in explaining to

the PAC[12] why two very senior ex-Foreign Office officials were now graded as junior assistants of the GC and CS.
5. In 1925 when we first recruited young staff direct from the university, the establishment was increased to 10 seniors and 20 juniors. But promotion was slow. Naturally there was little or no difference in the work of good juniors and seniors. Therefore during the early 1930s the proportion was altered to 15 seniors and 15 juniors.
6. But promotion was still too slow, principally because no seniors died nor were superannuated. Therefore in 1937 the Treasury agreed to promotion of junior to senior after 10 years' service and the scales were slightly altered and fixed at:
    junior assistants £250 – 25 – £500
    senior assistants £700 – 30 – £1,000
    chief assistants £1,000 – £1,100
while the head and deputy head were given the position and pay of assistant secretaries.
7. The above paragraphs (B, 1–6) have concerned the civil staff established under the Foreign Office. It might be fitting now briefly to account for the contribution made by the Services (Admiralty, War Office and [later] Air Ministry).
8. Their main effort was in the interception of foreign government W/T messages, a subject outside the scope of this paper. But the Admiralty and the War Office did make some staff contribution to the GC and CS until the time when the War Office and Air Ministry did maintain their own section within the framework of GC and CS.
9. From 1923 onwards the Admiralty evinced special interest in the Japanese diplomatic and naval attaché traffic and always provided one officer (Japanese interpreter) to work in the section. When a small party in the Far East was being formed, a system of rotation arose. Ultimately when in 1934 Admiralty started a bureau in Hongkong, sufficient officers had been trained to man it and Paymaster-Captain Shaw (then retired) was taken on the Foreign Office Establishment to act as the first head of the bureau. Further Admiralty assistance in the matter of staff is described in part C.

But the Admiralty, unlike the other two services, never maintained their own section in GC and CS.
10. The War Office, at the time of the Armistice, had in addition to MI 1B, certain small sections overseas of which the one in Constantinople continued to function after 1918 until its staff were transferred (about 1922) to form the original nucleus of the War Office station at Sarafand which still exists today as an intercepting and crypto-graphic unit dealing almost entirely with local problems. A close liaison between GC and CS and Sarafand has always been a

satisfactory feature. During the twenties the War Office did send military officers to GC and CS for some training before proceeding abroad. Among others, Captain Tiltman [13] spent some months in 1920 at Watergate House on his way to the Middle East. But it was not until the early troublous thirties that Captain Tiltman, having returned from a long tour of duty in India, rejoined us, and before long started, himself as a civilian under the War Office, the Military Section to which were attached an increasing number of military officers. Their activities will be described more fully in [part] C.

11. For at least 15 years of our life the Air Ministry, while considerably interested in some of our results, contented themselves with the provision of valuable intercepting facilities. But about 1936 their Intelligence authorities felt the need of a technical expert of their own. They therefore set up the RAF Section within the framework of GC and CS and Mr J.E.S. Cooper [14] was transferred from the Foreign Office to the Air Ministry civil establishment. The early development of this section will also be dealt with more fully in [part] C.

12. During 1937 the Admiral, convinced of the inevitability of war, gave instructions for the earmarking of the right type of recruit to reinforce GC and CS *immediately* on the outbreak of war.

    Through the Chief Clerk's Department we obtained Treasury sanction for 56 seniors, men or women, with the right background and training (salary £600 a year) and 30 girls with a graduate's knowledge of at least two of the languages required (£3 a week).

    To obtain such men and women I got in touch with all the universities. It was naturally at that time impossible to give details of the work, nor was it always advisable to insist too much in these circles on the imminence of war.

    At certain universities, however, there were men now in senior positions who had worked in our ranks during 1914–18. These men knew the type required. Thus it fell out that our most successful recruiting occurred from these universities. During 1937 and 1938 we were able to arrange a series of courses to which we invited our recruits to give them even a dim idea of what would be required of them.[15]

    This enabled our recruits to know the type of man and mind best fitted and they in turn could and did earmark, if only mentally, further suitable candidates. These men joined up in September 1939.

    Thus very early in the war GC and CS had collected a large body of suitable men and women quite apart from recruitment of service personnel by the two service sections, of which the Military was now on an entirely military footing.

13. With regard to the clerical and typing staff which grew gradually

during those years, involving us in prolonged discussions with the Treasury, the Tomlin Civil Service Commission of 1929 widened the basis of establishment, consequently we did obtain sanction for the establishment of two higher clerical, some six to ten clerical officers, about a dozen clerical assistants and half a dozen typists.

By this means were were able to retain with prospects of pension some of those girls and women who had proved their value to us in both our functions.

TOP SECRET

C [DEVELOPMENT 1919–1939]

1. In A,5 I stated that the ostensible function of GC and CS was 'to advise as to the security of codes and cyphers used by all government departments and to assist in their provision'.

This duty was carried out exclusively by Travis[16] who came to us fresh from this type of work in the Admiralty, together with a clerical party whom he had trained. He alone is in a position to tell the story of its development.

Suffice it to say that each of the big departments nominated officers in the Communications Branch to act in liaison with us. The Admiralty alone appointed an officer to work in GC and CS (later increased to two officers). Out of this has now grown the section known as CSA with far wider responsibility and power.

2. The secret side of GC and CS had as its task 'to study communications of foreign governments'.

The development of this work I propose to outline under the headings Diplomatic, Clandestine, Services and Commercial in the order of their appearance as vital issues during the period 1919–1939.

3. *Diplomatic*

As stated in A, 1 and 2, some diplomatic work was undertaken in both sections during the 1914–18 war. But it must be emphasised that this work was from a cryptographer's standpoint most elementary. Of the countries then tackled and read, only the German Foreign Office was using 'hat' books and reciphering methods: all the others read had an alphabetical basis. Sir George Young[17] invented a method of reading German hat books (for which he received a monetary reward) which included an elaborate card index manned by some ten graduate women. Within a year of the start of GC and CS, the solution of a hat book was the task of one good linguist working on the method used Mr Fetterlein for many years in this work in Russia. I myself, working with Young, also received a monetary reward for solving the first additive key we had ever seen as used by the Germans. When I say that this key varied from 7–13 digits, I must consider myself lucky to have been rewarded for a job which nowadays any young cryptographer would take in his stride.

Fetterlein's previous training enabled us to read the fairly complex Austrian keys and rebuild their hatted books.

It might perhaps be noted here that I took a small Admiralty party over to Paris, in April 1919, to work with the French on the *German* material passing during the Peace Conference. We remained until the signing of the Peace of Versailles and I have always thought that our visit was useless though pleasant. Although Germany was a beaten nation, nothing appeared in the terms of Armistice concerning their diplomatic cyphers. Consequently their mission came to Paris provided with entirely new books and methods. We obtained all the traffic between Paris and Berlin but failed to produce anything of any value. How could we? Germany knew well we had read her diplomatic traffic for the last three years (e.g. Zimmerman Letter),[18] and no one prevented Germany from replacing her compromised codes by the safest methods she could devise. I believe that at that time Germany made use of OTP[19] for the first time. I am certain she used the method ultimately solved in 1942 and then only thanks to an amazing scrap of physical compromise. In any case there was no GC and CS at that date and such was the lack of co-ordination that the party in Paris never saw results obtained in London of American and Japanese work, while French and Italian had then never been attempted.

All other powers which were read in wartime, including American, Japanese, Greek, Spanish and Scandinavian, were using alphabetical books. Norwegian was alphabetical; the first Danish and Swedish solved were hatted but some 'cribs'[20] were available.

Thus it came about that in 1919 only those who had worked on the enemy countries, who were driven to recyphering processes, had had any real experience in cryptography. The majority of the party were linguists. Ultimately the reconstruction of code books used and the translation and emendation of the resultant texts was our productive function. Fetterlein, Strachey[21] and Knox[22] were our original key men while Turner[23] had the role of master-linguist with Hobart-Hampden in charge of Japanese.

The first effort of the early years was devoted to breaking into the hitherto untouched material from various governments.

a. The Americans celebrated the advent of peace by introducing a new hatted diplomatic code recyphered with tables changing quarterly. The solution of the first of these tables was a year's work and thereafter the American Section had to be expanded for the increased task of breaking the tables and reconstructing the code. Good progress was made, and the section was able to be of some assistance during the Washington Naval Conference in 1922.

b. The second really big task was to make a concentrated attack on

French diplomatic cyphers, which had received no attention during the war.

A large number of hatted books of 10,000 groups were used and with the constant practice of reconstruction of such books they never presented any difficulty. Given sufficient traffic, legibility appeared within a month of birth.

Many recyphered books also appeared and after the initial struggle to obtain the general system the constant change of tables presented little difficulty. Only about 1935 did the French introduce any system which defied solution. This was a development of the bigrammatic substitution and it was felt that even this would not be insoluble if only there were enough traffic. The Quai d'Orsay is conservative and we never observed anything of the OTP type.

The reading of this traffic during the years of peace and intrigue did from time to time produce very interesting if not invaluable intelligence. But the proximity of the two capitals did mean that a great deal passed by bag.

c. The only real operational intelligence came from our work on the Soviet traffic. We were able to attack their systems step by step with success from the days of Litvinov's first visit to Copenhagen, of Kamenev as their first representative in London followed by Krassin, until the famous Arcos Raid in 1927 (?)[24] when HMG found it necessary to compromise our work beyond any question. From that time the Soviet government introduced OTP for their diplomatic and commercial traffic to all capitals where they had diplomatic representatives.

The revolutionary government in 1919 had no codes and did not risk using the Czarist codes which they must have inherited. They began with simple transposition of plain Russian and gradually developed systems of increasing difficulty. The presence of Fetterlein as a senior member of the staff and two very competent girls, refugees from Russia, with a perfect knowledge of the language, who subsequently became permanent members of the staff, enabled us to succeed in this work. We were also able to borrow certain British Consuls who could not return to Russia.

d. The fourth big productive effort was on the Japanese. Here the cryptographic task was for the first ten years almost non-existent so far as diplomatic work was concerned. For the language, which was the main difficulty, we were lucky enough to have recruited Hobart-Hampden just retired from 30 years' service in the East. But for a long time he was virtually alone, but with his knowledge of the habits of the Japanese he soon acquired an uncanny skill in never missing the important. Probably not more than 20 per cent of the traffic received was circulated, but throughout the period down to 1931 no big conference was held in Washington, London or Geneva in which he did not contribute all the views of the Japanese government and of their too verbose representatives. Sir Harold Parlett,[25] another distinguished officer from the Japanese service, joined him in 1926 and ably seconded him with an equal sense of the essential. Yardley's 'Black Chamber' tells of the American success at the Washington Conference.[26] No one will ever tell how much accurate and reliable information was made available to our Foreign Office and Service Departments during those critical years.

Of the building up of the Japanese naval work, in which both these officers played a part, I will be speaking briefly later.

e.   A continued watch was kept on the ex-enemy countries, but here there was little development. Germany was allowed to introduce her new methods, and we soon knew that she was using OTP for all she wished to keep secret. In course of time we knew her method of using pads and how she made them up. We also knew of her second method and diagnosed it as unbreakable.

This second method, nicknamed Floradora, was finally broken in 1942 thanks to three chances:

1. The basic book fell into our hands;
2. Close co-operation with USA;
3. SS[27] work by an able ally who obtained first-hand information and one page of figures from a German cypher officer.

We had in fact reconstructed the basic book during the period 1932–39, but the effort was never profitable as German security rules forbade its use unrecyphered, except for purely administrative telegrams which proved of little interest or value.

The Austrian government had always used reasonably secure methods of recypherment and never used their books plain. Thanks to assistance from Fetterlein we did read them in 1918 and 1919, as there was sufficient traffic. But Trianon[28] produced a small poor country whose communications grew less and less, and ultimately we failed for lack of telegrams.

Austria, Hungary, and the Balkan countries rarely produced sufficient material to justify an attack. The greater part of their telegrams probably passed on the continental landlines which were never available to use in peace.

Hungarian was successfully tackled by Knox, but it is doubtful if the results obtained at that time justified the enormous effort on his part.

Later an increase in the use of W/T[29] and the troublous political situation did enable us to read some of the traffic of these countries but never have we been able to report full legibility, a regular flow of traffic and valuable results.

f.   Some of the other powers had already been started in MI 1B or 40 OB, notably Greek, Spanish, Italian, Scandinavian and Persian and where purely alphabetical books were used, telegrams had been read and circulated.

Sections were therefore formed in the new GC and CS to carry on this work. Early in our career the Foreign Office disclaimed any interest in Scandinavian, so this subject was dropped.

Passage of time and changes in the political situation opened up new lines. The various South American republics, Portuguese, Brazilian, were tackled. The Balkans were watched, though little traffic was available as European landlines carried most of it. A Near East Section was envisaged, working in close co-operation with the military station at Sarafand, of which I will write later.

To sum up the cryptographic effort of 20 years on diplomatic traffic: we started in 1919 at the period of bow-and-arrow methods, i.e., alphabetic books; we followed the various developments of security measures adopted in every country; we reached 1939 with a full knowledge of all the methods evolved, and with the ability to read all diplomatic communications of all powers except those which had been forced, like Germany and Russia, to adopt OTP.

The authority who sanctioned our establishment in 1919 clearly never envisaged a complete reading, translation and issue of every telegram received by us.

Such was a physical impossibility for the 30 specialists who composed the main body of the staff employed on the work.

Hence from the outset sections did exercise their own discretion as to what they translated and submitted for circulation. They got guidance from the D and R who in turn received intelligence directives from the Foreign Office, the circulating sections of SIS and the officers who used our material in the Service and other large departments.

During the thirties we did supplement our daily issue by a daily 'Summary of telegrams decoded but not circulated', for the benefit of SIS, Admiralty and War Office (occasionally the Foreign Office) and it is noteworthy that it was only a very small percentage that were ever asked for in complete form.

With personal satisfaction I maintain that GC and CS did during those 20 years fulfil its allotted function with success, with exiguous numbers and with an absence of publicity which greatly enhanced the value of its work.

4. *Clandestine*

Peacetime GC and CS did have one experience of successful work on clandestine traffic. This, unlike the diplomatic, necessitated close co-operation between interception, T/A[30] and cryptography before the final results were made available only to a small select intelligence section of SIS.

Some time around 1930 our stations picked up a mass of unusual and unkown transmissions, all in cypher except for the 'operators' chat', which was all of the international amateur type.

The analysis of this traffic was studied closely, and from it emerged a worldwide network of clandestine stations controlled by a station near Moscow. It turned out to be the Comintern network. Brigadier Tiltman has written up the story of the cryptography attack which met with complete success.[31] Control of interception, including D/F,[32] was left to Kenworthy[33] and Lambert,[34] and their successful effort to locate a room in a house in a terrace in a suburb of London was perhaps the earliest example of this type of work, and proved in the early days the value of co-operation between interception, T/A and cryptography.

I can imagine that there was a considerable amount of clandestine wireless from 1935 onwards, during the Abyssinian and Spanish wars, and various episodes of Hitler's aggression, but lack of technical facilities prevented any attempt at interception.

One other clandestine network was observed and studied by us in the prewar days, namely that organised by the German Foreign Office. As we were aware that already our own Foreign Office and SIS were taking steps to ensure communications with our embassies and posts abroad in the event of a breakdown of the normal routes, we were not surprised when Denmark Hill in 1937 and 1938 obtained obvious German diplomatic traffic broadcast from an unlisted station in Germany to unknown recipient call-signs as well as obvious replies from unknown stations.

As previously stated, we could not read the traffic, but it could not be mistaken: it was not disguised. Interception, T/A and direction finding enabled us, even in those days, to be certain that every German embassy and legation and many German consulates were equipped with W/T gear for reception *and* transmission. Denmark Hill was able to make preliminary studies of all the methods of changing frequencies, call-signs, etc, used to disguise as far as possible the originators and the services, so as to avoid interception and identification. When later during the war it became necessary to obtain all this material, these early studies by Denmark Hill proved of very great help.

5. *Services*

GC and CS, as an office, had no means of obtaining W/T traffic. Admiralty and War Office had set up a large number of intercepting stations during the war, from which DNI (Admiral Sinclair) persuaded the Signal Department to retain two, Scarborough and Pembroke, and the Military Directorate in the War Office to retain one at Chatham. Naturally the first duty of these stations was to watch the service traffic of other powers, but they also undertook to spend part of their time watching the big commercial transmitters in foreign countries with a view to obtaining such government cypher traffic as they heard. I propose to go more fully into this question in section D. But it had to be mentioned here as one reason for the creation of a Naval Section.

Admiralty. The beginning of the Naval Section is obscure in my memory. Clarke,[35] who became the head of the section, did not join until 1921 as he was engaged in writing up the naval history of the Great War. But the Admiralty did lend certain officers, first German, then Italian linguists. There was of course very little German naval material in the early years: there was no German navy to speak of. There was a small amount, but it was soon apparent that we could not read it. The Armistice Commission and the Peace Treaty had made no demands. So far as I remember we concluded that a machine recypher had been applied to the 4-letter code book with which the German navy finished the war, but at that time we knew nothing of the German development of the Enigma machine. It is possible that in 1923–25 they were already using it.

In any case there was no navy, and consequently little traffic, and so interception was dropped.

The Italian navy was also watched, and here we were lucky. There was a navy and consequently a fair amount of traffic, and in early days we did reconstruct the main naval code book because of the delightful Italian habit of encyphering long political leaders from the daily press. As can be imagined in those years and with such habits, the Intelligence value of the effort was slight, but we did build a foundation which proved of value from 1934 onwards.

But even in the early twenties the Admiralty did evince an interest in Japan. But GC and CS only obtained diplomatic and attaché material – no Japanese naval traffic could be intercepted in this country. We knew the Japanese cryptographic methods to be low-grade – the language was the difficulty and linguists were hard to find. The Admiralty, however, had a certain number of interpreters, some of whom were for one reason or another no longer essential for active service. From 1922 onwards we had always one naval officer working in the Japanese Section, reading the diplomatic and naval attaché telegrams. By 1925 we even had officers still on the active list and a scheme was arranged whereby such came to us for two years and then joined the China Squadron in a ship where there were facilities for local interception. Thus a first start was made on Japanese naval traffic.

From then onwards there was a flow of traffic by bag to London where the various codes were segregated and broken as far as possible, and a return flow of officers with skeleton books to carry on the work locally. I believe that by 1930 they were able to be of definite use to the C-in-C, China. Finally the Admiralty sent out Captain Tait (then DDNI) to study the Far East question, and in consequence of his report, set up a small bureau for interception and cryptography at Hongkong (moved to Singapore in September 1939) where Captain Shaw, now retired, headed the first party to exploit Japanese naval signals, to which was added the beginning of Japanese military. The Diplomatic Section had followed the diplomatic and attaché developments, including the introduction of mechanical devices, successfully, and thus it can be maintained that in early 1939, GC and CS had full control of diplomatic and attaché traffic, were reasonably fluent in their reading of all the main naval cyphers and knew quite a lot about Japanese army cyphers as used in China.

To revert to European affairs, the period of dull slackness of naval affairs and traffic, noted in the opening paragraphs of this section, continued with slight alarms and excursions consequent upon naval reviews and vists until around about 1934, when the Italian governments probably began to plan the Abyssinian Campaign. From then onwards, Italian naval traffic was obtained in increasing quantity with increased security measures. The section kept pace with it all, though by 1935 increased numbers and more room had to be provided. Throughout the campaign and in the tenser moments aroused by the threat of sanctions, the section were able to keep DNI fully informed of the strength and activities of the Italian navy. When in the Spanish war the Italians, not content with their own reasonably secure hand methods, introduced the commercial Enigma machine for all their secret naval communications, this proved a heaven-sent opportunity for us to explore machine encypherment. Knox led the party and younger men, such as Bodsworth[36] and Twinn,[37] had their first experience with him, a fact which proved invaluable after 1939.

It was not until the summer of 1936 that any interest was taken in the German navy. But when they appeared that year in the Mediterranean, all our stations were inundated with frequent repetitions of their naval broadcasts. Work began at once under Knox and by this time we were quite aware that the Enigma machine, with the special attachment known as the 'Stecker', was the basis of their service signals. Strong efforts were also made by out naval stations to supplement the broadcasts by ship signals and local coast stations in Germany to try to find lower grade traffic. Lack of gear and men prevented this. Knox made considerable progress in his diagnosis until April 1937, when the Germans introduced the new method of indication [4 bigrams] to which he had to admit defeat. Captures in the spring of 1940 showed the correctness of this diagnosis. In 1937 we had no access to mechanical devices which alone enabled this system of indication to be overcome.

But correct diagnosis does not read messages, so the German naval signals were submitted to another process which we called W/T from which we hoped to learn something of German naval activities. Even in the Great War during 1917 and 1918, when new books were introduced and the cryptographers of 40 OB were not in production, the 'plotting' section, with the unread signals before them, did continue to produce daily a reasonably accurate situation report. But no German naval signals had been read for 20 years, and it was hardly to be hoped that the Nazi German navy had preserved the habits and routines of the imperial navy. Nevertheless, from 1937 onwards, such an effort was made by officers lent to GC and CS by the Admiralty, reinforced by available members of GC and CS. We had no accurate checks by the cyphers becoming legible; but out of this effort grew the art now called, I think, T/A, which from 1940 onwards has proved a most valuable adjunct to cryptography, quite capable of acting as a trustworthy substitute when the cryptographer is temporarily unproductive.

To sum up the situation of the Naval Section in 1939, including the Japanese branch in Hongkong: they exercised a very fair measure of control of all Italian and Japanese naval cyphers; they had only seen German signals by the Enigma machine and this they could not read; they had started an intensive professional study of raw German traffic with a view to extracting any available intelligence.

Military Unlike the NID, MI 1 always maintained a personal interest, not only in interception and result but also in cryptography. Before there was any question of a Military Section, officers were sent to us with the definite object of training, while the Admiralty lent officers to assist us in producing results. As stated above, the War Office had, during the war, maintained posts abroad, and early in the twenties decided to set up a permanent intercepting station in the Middle East, and about 1923 Sarafand in Palestine was selected and started to function. In addition to interception, they also intended to read the traffic which affected the area. Therefore at Sarafand Arabic was a primary concern, while French and later Italian were also exploited. I visited there in 1925 and am glad to think that the liaison between GC and CS and Sarafand has been maintained for 20 years. Many army officers worked in both places. MI 1 was also our liaison with a bureau which the Indian army had founded during the war to handle the problems (Persian, Afghan, Russian) which affected India.

Throughout the twenties the military officers who joined us went to sections where their language was used or in which the War Office was interested, because there was *no purely military* traffic. But very early in the thirties the War Office decided to regularise this somewhat haphazard form of training, and the Military Section was formed to which all army officers with us were attached. Tiltman was made the head of the section, receiving the position of senior assistant on the War Office civil establishment. Members of the Military Section conformed to the routine and discipline of the GC and CS, but MI 1 had the right to dictate their requirements as to training and type of work. At a later date the War Office also recruited civilians on the same lines as GC and CS. Thus was laid the foundation of the very large Military Wing of the war period. Originally the Military Section took over certain of the normal commitments of GC and CS, but with the increasing threat of war, gradually the subject and the traffic on which the sections work[ed] became more definitely military. The Far East began to send back bags of Japanese military material, the Japanese military attachés in Europe began to assume importance. Then the Abyssinian and Spanish wars produced large quantities of Italian military material. All of this latter was tackled successfully, and consequently the section became well trained to face their operational task in 1940.

Naturally the Military Section worked in close co-operation with the military intercepting station at Chatham, and it was thanks to this that the section, and GC and CS as a whole, had, in 1937, their first glimpse of German army and air force material, and of German police transmissions. Knox failed in his effort on the naval enigma, led the team which started to investigate this new problem. Tiltman, deep in other problems, broke in to contribute one vital link. An ever closer liaison with the French, and through them with the Poles, stimulated the attack. Fresh ideas flowed, even from those selected from a university as recruits in the event of war. I think it may be rightly held that this effort of 1938 and 1939 enabled the party at B/P [38] to read the current traffic of the GAF [39] within five months of the outbreak of war.

RAF Section The Air Ministry had, since 1922, contributed to our need for traffic by maintaining a very good intercepting station at Waddington. There was no real air traffic, so we profited. As the Intelligence Division of the Air Ministry was never so politically minded as in the other two services, our diplomatic result could not have had the same value to them. Our debt to them was therefore the larger. But with the threat of war, about 1935 the Air Ministry decided to form an Air Section to work in GC and CS on the lines of the Military Section. They had no trained experts of their own. They asked, therefore, to have a member of GC and CS transferred to their civil establishment. So Cooper became the first head of the RAF Section and I am sure that the Air Ministry will agree that GC and CS repaid their earlier debt to the full, and with interest. In 1938 further civilians were recruited direct into the section.

From then onwards, Cheadle, whither Waddington had transferred, began to look out for foreign air traffic.

The war in Spain and aggression in Europe gave them ample scope. Italians, Spanish and German operational air-to-ground was collected and worked on with success. So the section had first-hand knowledge of some of the methods used by the Germans when war began.

6 Commercial

For 20 years, during which cable companies submitted all their traffic to the GC and CS, a vast number of telegrams of a purely commercial nature were seen but never copied. Similarly, the operators at the intercepting stations had to hear and pass over far more than they recorded. We only worked on foreign government traffic. Once or twice perhaps we may have looked out for individuals. Once most certainly we did investigate the telegrams of certain oil companies. But this was not our function. In those days of peace, all companies of any repute had their private codes or at least private encypherments of standard commercial codes. Apart from secrecy, it is cheaper to use code for telegrams. The majority of these commercial codes can be purchased in the open market, whatever their nationality. Therefore the reading of such telegrams presents no difficulty, and where encyphered, GC and CS should be able to break it down.

But with the few exceptions noted above, commercial work was not in our mandate and we had not the necessary staff.

Sometime in 1938 the Admiral and the newly appointed DNI [40] formed that opinion that in the events of a troublous political situation in the Far East, the Japanese might take steps to render their diplomatic and service material illegible, and that the communications of the big Japanese firms, particularly as to shipping, might be the only available source of intelligence.

Further, Major Desmond Morton had now organised a section known as IIC [41] for the study of commercial and financial intelligence out of which grew MEW [42] in the latter half of 1939. He was on our circulating list and was always anxious to extend the bases of his intelligence.

Therefore, in 1938, Hope [42] started a very small section to investigate commercial traffic, more especially the telegrams of the big Japanese firms. A library of all the known commercial codes in various languages was assembled as a necessary foundation. But his task was definitely cryptographic.

About this time the Cable Censorship were engaged in drafting their final plans. They naturally intended to stop the use of code for all terminal traffic (except of course for neutral and allied governments whose representatives enjoy cipher privilege). Consequently the Censors themselves would circulate the intelligence derived from terminal plain language. But they did not propose to interfere with traffic transit at censorship points, and they agreed to provide our commercial section with all the commercial code telegrams of this nature. Our intercepting stations were now, in late 1938, asked to record commercial traffic where possible, and as much of this was taken on high speed automatic gear, our slipreading party had even then to be reinforced. The Commercial Section did have 12 months' experience of a variety of the codes used by all nations, including Japanese, and of the type and mass of plain language commercial telegrams. Above all they began to learn the very necessary discriminations. Never more than 10 per cent of the very large numbers of telegrams received really justified translation and circulation and the accurate selection of this 16 per cent required training and close liaison with the users.

SUPPLEMENT

TRAFFIC

The Cabinet authority establishing GC and CS gave no directive as to raw material, without which little could be done. But the authorities controlling the new body were fully alive to the necessity and supported to the best of their power all suggestions we put forward. We only had the experience of four years of war, when such a question was simple, because our results were valued.

Full cable censorship provided copies of all cable traffic. The development of the scientific methods of intercepting W/T traffic, service or commercial, dated only from 1914 but was now practised on a considerable scale by stations controlled by Admiralty, War Office and GPO. It was necessary to ensure that the provision both of cable and W/T traffic should continue under peace conditions.

1. *Cables*

The conclusion of the Treaty meant the suspension of censorship. Temporary unofficial arrangements were made with the moribund censors which provided the cable traffic for some further months. But legislation in the form of the Official Secrets Act gave the government the right to obtain cable traffic for scrutiny purposes *not* for censorship. A clause was inserted authorising a secretary of state to issue a warrant to cable companies operating in the UK requiring these companies to hand over all traffic passing over their systems in the UK within ten days of receipt or despatch to a named department, for the purpose of scrutiny, the secretary of state alleging that a general state of unrest and world emergency required him to make this demand.

I believe the Secretary of State for Home Affairs signed the original warrant and named the Admiralty. I believe occasional questions were asked in the House but we continued to receive *all* cable traffic from all the companies until September 1939, when cable censorship was again instituted, and once again the Censors provided us through the war with copies of the traffic we asked for.

Throughout the 20 years (1919–39) it was our aim to make this procedure work smoothly with the companies (British and foreign). It was undoubtedly a nuisance for them to have to send all their traffic in sacks to an outside department, and I have always considered that the credit for smooth working and no questioning should go to Maine.[44] To carry out the work of sorting and copying we took over a comparatively small body of GPO lower grade staff who were accustomed to this work. Our aim was to inconvenience the companies as little as possible, and throughout we tried to let them have their traffic back within 24 hours. We only had to sort out and copy government traffic and occasional suspicious characters in whom our security authorities were interested. I believe we never failed to return all the traffic, though many million telegrams must have passed through our hands.

Another very valuable job carried out by Maine was to obtain traffic from stations abroad where, during the war, there had been a censorship point, e.g. Malta, Hongkong, Bermuda. Traffic at these points was *not* required under the warrant.

Malta, above all, the focal point for traffic between Europe and all the East, was of the highest importance. Maine was able to arrange with Messrs Cable and Wireless, who operated the stations, that they should have all the slip transmitting Malta sent back by bag to London, ostensibly for accountancy purposes. We received it, engaged slipreaders, and had this valuable material regularly, though of course with a considerable delay. For instance, the Japanese traffic to France and Germany always went via Malta. All Italian cable traffic passed there. Thus we were, throughout, enabled to watch the growth of the Axis combination.

In a similar way we were able to watch other old censorship points and, finding the traffic of little value, to give them up again.

It is probable that once again after this war, Malta traffic will be essential.

Also, with the CTO,[45] Maine's excellent liaison proved of the greatest help at times when foreign embassies during big conferences requested and obtained private lines from their embassy to their capital. The Germans, the French and other great powers adopted this procedure on occasions. Of course these private lines had to pass through the CTO, and Maine was always able to arrange for measures to be taken there whereby copies became available to us.

Finally, when the state of unrest in the world became intense, from 1935 onwards, it was found that the 10 days' delay granted by the warrant became intolerable. Maine was able to cut it down to 24–48 hours in the case of foreign companies, and to instant service, where necessary, in the case of the CTO and Cable and Wireless.

Between us and the companies there has never been any question as to why we wanted the traffic and what we did with it. The warrant merely said scrutiny, and the traffic arrived back apparently untouched within a few hours. I have no doubt that the managers and senior officials must have guessed the true answer, but I have never heard of any indiscretions through all these years with so many people involved.

In short, barring the delay, we always had as good service of cables when we dealt direct with the companies as in the periods of censorship.

2. W/T

We started the peace regime with two Admiralty stations, Pembroke and Scarborough, gradually decreasing their naval work owing to absence of targets and increasing their watch of the big foreign commercial stations, and thereby producing foreign government cipher traffic, and (in the early days) a good deal of foreign government P/L,[46] especially from Moscow.

Our director was at that time the DNI, Admiral Sinclair, who was obviously able to obtain the willing assistance of the Signal Department who owned the stations and the gear, and of ACR who provided the operators. Further, a Cabinet committee for postwar planning with General Romer as chairman had apparently planned for further interception and had appointed Admiral Sinclair as Co-ordinator of W/T interception. Before the Admiral left (in 1921) to take up the post of OC Submarines, naval interception by these stations was on a firm, if modest, footing, complicated only by the fact that ACR controlled the staff, DSD was responsible for station and sets, and DNI had to indicate the programme of work.[47]

About this time (1921) the WO also set up a station at Chatham under MI 1B, who were also prepared to produce material for us. The GSO2 or 3 of MI 1B became a liaison officer to GC and CS, and we worked out a plan of interception with him. Later (about 1923, I think) the Air Ministry joined up also and founded a station at Waddington under AII,[48] who also nominated a liaison officer to us. So, when the Admiral returned in 1924 as Director, there did exist a means of co-ordination on a low level, that is, such sets and operators as existed were used to our best advantage but any expansion was out of the question. He resumed his function as Chairman of the Co-ordinating Committee and held an annual meeting of the Directors of Intelligence at which on each occasion the Head of GC and CS and the liaison officers assisted. At the early meetings little could be done beyond allotting priorities of work as still no expansion could be hoped for.[49]

One of the first major actions the Admiral undertook was to arrange with the Police Commissioner for the loan of a small body of constables whom the Commissioner had used as a police W/T unit, I think, for interception of illicit transmissions in this country and for control of the police W/T network in London. These constables (10 to 12) had a small station at Denmark Hill, where their work was directed by a civilian engineer on the staff of the Receiver, Kenworthy by name. The Admiral undertook to pay for these men and the upkeep of the station while the Commissioner agreed to ask no questions about their work. This was the first station which undertook purely diplomatic work over which GC and CS had full control. It was soon apparent that Kenworthy possessed a flair for this work which amounted to genius. To him the FO and the Service intercepting authorities owe a very great debt, not only as a technical W/T engineer designing and constructing suitable gear, but also as the instructor in the matter of interception of difficult transmissions, and as a pioneer in the interception of non-Morse transmissions.

About 1929 the Admiralty began to take the Far East situation more seriously. The Committee of Co-ordination was able, not only to advise, but also to use the prestige of its members to force necessary expansion through the various departments. The Committee became known as the 'Y'[50] Committee, and they formed a 'Y Sub-Committee', consisting of the head of GC and CS and the liaison officers. This sub-committee from then onwards met once a fortnight in the GC and CS. Its terms of reference were: to study the work of the various stations, to co-ordinate the programmes allotted, to avoid waste of effort and to investigate new lines of traffic and new means of transmission. Thus policy and expansion were the functions of the 'Y' Committee, while the sub-committee formed the executive, each member reporting if need be, to his own director.

This continued smoothly until about 1935. Certain other departments were asked to appoint liaison officers who sat on the sub-committee, notably the GPO with whom we had hitherto little contact, the chairman of the W/T board, and later Gambier Parry[51] (then Captain) who had been appointed as Section VIII of SIS.

From the beginning of the Abyssinian war the sub-committee began to take a far more active part, and co-ordination of programmes became a more difficult problem, because there was now service material to be intercepted and new service sections to study the traffic. Consequently, fewer sets were now available for diplomatic traffic at a time when the contents were of more vital interest.

With the best will in the world, the service officers could hardly make a case for expansion on behalf of diplomatic traffic. It was possible for the Admiral to persuade the Commissioner to increase the staff at Denmark Hill, but with the increase of world unrest, it became clear that the FO would have to take its share in interception. Protracted negotiations resulted in success, but it was not until 11 September 1939 that the first station was opened at Sandridge. It had been planned and erected by the GPO. All the gear was designed and provided by the GPO engineering branch and the operators were all GPO staff. The FO footed the bill and GC and CS directed the various programmes of work. This very important development was one of the major actions of the sub-committee.

Another was the introduction of teleprinter links between the stations and GC and CS. Hitherto all traffic arrived by registered post creating an average delay of twelve hours. During the anxious days of the Spanish war it had become obvious that all delays must be cut down, and the service members were able to use the value of the results to induce their authorities to sanction the installation of the T/P[52] links between GC and CS and the naval stations (Flowerdown and Scarborough), the WO station (Chatham) and the RAF station (Cheadle). Of course, not only service material but also diplomatic was passed over these links. Thus we had two years' experience of rapid and efficient communication.

In the spring of 1938 the Admiral bought the property at Bletchley Park, and the GPO set to work to equip it with suitable lines of communications. In the autumn of that year the service sections of GC and CS spent a month at the Park simulating, as far as possible, wartime conditions and direct communication. Thus it fell out that our work could definitely begin on 1 August 1939, when the Admiral ordered the service sections to take up their war stations. The diplomatic and commercial sections were ordered to move on 15 August.

From then onwards the university recruits began to join, so that by 1 September when war was declared,[52] GC and CS was in action at its war station, already in process of growth towards that vast and successful body whose full story will perhaps never be told.

2 December 1944

NOTES

*Alastair Denniston's original typescript, published here by kind permission of his son Robin, contains neither title nor notes. Both have been added by the Editor. The subheads A, B, C refer to the sections originally labelled a), b), c).

1. Later Sir Eric Jones, director of GCHQ, 1956–60; his memorandum is still classified.
2. Admiral Sir Hugh 'Quex' Sinclair, Head of the Secret Service (SIS) and (non-operational) Director of GC & CS, 1923–39.
3. Better known as Room 40 OB; the suffix refers to the Admiralty Old Building.
4. Sinclair was Director of Naval Intelligence, 1919–21.
5. Of 1920.
6. Cuts in government expenditure recommended by the committee headed by Sir Eric Geddes.
7. 1 Melbury Road, W14 was then the HQ of the Secret Intelligence Service (SIS), headed until his death in June 1923 by Captain Sir Mansfield Cumming, RN.
8. SIS and GC & CS.

THE GC & CS BETWEEN THE WARS

9. 54 Broadway, opposite St. James's Park tube station.
10. Ernest Hobart-Hampden, former consul in China and Japan.
11. E. C. Fetterlein, a former Tsarist cryptanalyst, now head of the Russian Section of GC & CS. See the article above by Andrew and Neilson.
12. Public Accounts Committee.
13. Later Brigadier John H. Tiltman, head of the Military Section in GC & CS.
14. 'Josh' Cooper, head of the Air Force Section in GC & CS.
15. On this recruitment see Christopher Andrew, 'F. H. Hinsley and the Cambridge Moles; Two Patterns of Intelligence Recruitment', in Richard Langhorne (ed.), *Diplomacy and Intelligence during the Second World War* (Cambridge, 1985).
16. Later Sir Edward Travis, director of GCHQ 1942–52.
17. Former diplomat and head of the Diplomatic Section of Room 40.
18. In fact the telegram from Arthur Zimmermann, German foreign minister, to the German minister in Mexico City on 16 January 1917, decrypted by Room 40. For two recent discussions of this episode see Patrick Beesly, *Room 40*, (London, 1982) Chapter 13, and Christopher Andrew, *Secret Service: The Making of the British Intelligence Community* (London, 1985), Chapter 3.
19. One-Time Pad.
20. On 'cribs' see the article below by Christopher Morris.
21. Oliver Strachey, formerly of MI1b, later head of ISOS (Intelligence Services Oliver Strachey) at Bletchley Park.
22. Dillwyn 'Dilly' Knox, former Fellow of King's College, Cambridge, probably Room 40's ablest codebreaker and later head of ISK (Intelligence Services Knox) at Bletchley Park.
23. J. Turner, a founder-member of GC & CS: I have been unable to discover his background. Unlike Fetterlein, Strachey and Knox, he did not survive into the Bletchley Park era.
24. The Special Branch raid on the London Offices of ARCOS (the All-Russian Co-operative Society), of whose date Denniston was uncertain, did indeed take place in 1927. It was quickly followed by the breaking of Anglo-Soviet diplomatic relations and the government's revelation that Britain had broken Soviet codes. On the attack on Soviet traffic up to 1927 see Andrew, *Secret Service*, Chapters 9, 10.
25. Previously Japanese counsellor at the Tokyo embassy.
26. After being dismissed as head of the Black Chamber (the American GC & CS) in 1929, Herbert Hardley wrote *The American Black Chamber* (New York, 1931) which described, *inter alia*, the breaking of Japanese codes during the Washington conference in 1921.
27. Secret Service.
28. The peace treaty of Trianon with Hungary on June 1920; Denniston probably confused this treaty with the peace treaty of St. Germain of September 1919 between the allies and the Austrian Republic.
29. Wireless Telegraphy.
30. Traffic Analysis.
31. Tiltman's account is still classified. See Andrew, *Secret Service*, pp. 365 ff.
32. Direction Finding.
33. An engineer who directed a small police W/T station at Denmark Hill in London; his work is further described below.
34. Leslie H. Lambert, a founder member of GC & CS and, under the pseudonym 'A. J. Alan', a popular radio story-teller.
35. Paymaster Lieutenant-Commander William F. 'Nobby' Clarke RNVR, a veteran of Room 40.
36. Wilfred Bodsworth, later head of cipher work in the Naval Section.
37. Peter Twinn, later Knox's successor as head of ISK at Bletchley Park.
38. Bletchley Park.
39. German air force.
40. Admiral John H. Godfrey, who took office as DNI in January 1939.
41. Industrial Intelligence Centre.

42. Ministry of Economic Warfare.
43. G.L.N. Hope, a veteran of Room 40 and founder member of GC & CS.
44. H.C.S. Maine, a founder member of GC & CS.
45. Central Telegraph Office.
46. Plain Language.
47. There is some material on the work of the Romer Committee and the subsequent organisation of W/T interception in PRO WO 32/4897.
48. Section I of Air Intelligence.
49. See 'Report of the Inter-Service Directorate Committee' and subsequent correspondence in PRO WO 32/4897.
50. Radio-interception.
51. Later Brigadier Richard Gambier Parry, head of the Communications Section in SIS.
52. Teleprinter.
53. Germany invaded Poland on 1 September 1939. Britain declared war two days later.

From Polish Bomba to British Bombe: The Birth of Ultra

GORDON WELCHMAN

I

THE POLES, THE BRITISH AND THE FRENCH

Until just before the Second World War a small Polish team of three mathematician-cryptologists, headed by the brilliant Marian Rejewski, had been happily breaking the German military cipher machine, the Enigma, for many years. A small British team under the First World War cryptanalyst, Dilly Knox, was near to success, but was foiled by failure to make a guess which, in retrospect, seems an obvious one. The French cryptanalysts do not appear to have tried, but Captain Gustave Bertrand, involved in French espionage, achieved a coup without which the Polish breaks and the subsequent British successes might never have been achieved.

The Poles kept their secret to themselves until July 1939 when, with the German invasion of their country imminent, they gave all their knowledge, as well as working replicas of the Enigma machine, to the French and British. In England, at Bletchley Park, we were quick to exploit the golden opportunity that the Poles had handed us. In France Bertrand established an organisation near Paris, code-named Bruno, at which Marian Rejewski and his associates Henryk Zygalski and Jerzy Rozycki, having escaped from Poland, continued to work on Enigma. There was collaboration between Bletchley and Bruno until the German advance on Paris forced an evacuation.

Ultra intelligence, based on decodes of the Enigma traffic of the German army and air force, was born early in 1940. Its heyday started after the battles of El Alamein and Stalingrad in the autumn of 1942 and the Allied landing in North Africa in November 1942. By that time the Allies had become strong enough to take advantage of this extraordinarily prolific source of intelligence, and a satisfactory means of sending Ultra information to commanders in the field had been developed.

As early as 1941 and 1942 Rejewski wrote reports in Polish on the pre-war breaking of the Enigma cipher. More than 30 years later, in 1973, Bertrand, infuriated by the publication of a completely erroneous account, decided to break silence. He published a book revealing that Enigma had been broken during the war.[1] This book, however, was not reviewed in any important periodical and sold very badly. The publication of Winterbotham's book, *The Ultra Secret*,[2] in 1974 was a very different story. Awareness of the major contribution that Ultra had made to Allied victory spread rapidly around the world. It is ironical that the editor of a French translation of Winterbotham's book had no idea of the existence of Bertrand's publication.

Since 1974 a great deal has been written about Ultra and many misconceptions have arisen. I myself, as author of *The Hut Six Story*,[3] have given rise to some of these. When I arrived at Bletchley Park in September 1939, Dilly Knox told me nothing about how the Poles had acquired the knowledge that they passed on to us. I had not even appreciated our debt to Rejewski until Professor Stengers sent me a copy of his paper in the February 1981 issue of *L'Histoire*.[4] With my book going to press a few months later, all I could do was make minor additions in the text and pay tribute to Rejewski in the dedication. Although Jozef Garlinski's book *The Enigma War*[5] was published in the USA in 1980, I did not hear of it in time to take advantage of the appendix by Colonel Tadeusz Lisicki, which contains an account of Rejewski's achievements.

The January 1982 issue of *Cryptologia* contained a translation of an article by Rejewski himself,[6] together with other information about his work. The April 1982 issue reviewed another article by Rejewski that had been published in *The Annals of the History of Computing*.[7] Two years later, an article by Professor Jean Stengers, 'Enigma, The French, the Poles and the British, 1931–1940' was published in England as part of *The Missing Dimension*, edited by Christopher Andrew and David Dilks.[8] Another book published in 1984 was *Enigma* by Wladyslaw Kozaczuk, edited and translated by Christopher Kasparek,[9] which appears to be an updated version of a book published in Polish in 1979.[10] It contains, as appendices, copies of all but one of the Rejewski articles that appeared in *Cryptologia*. Its last appendix contains many lengthy quotations from my book, *The Hut Six Story*.

The time has come to deal with many misconceptions that have arisen in these and other writings; particularly in Appendix 1 of Volume 1 of the official history of *British Intelligence in the Second World War*.[11] For example, a careful study of Rejewski's writings shows that the 'Bomba' was not as important as it has been made out to be. It had its brief day of glory, but was already ineffective when the Poles got us off to a flying start by telling us their secrets in July 1939. It would have been of no use to us, as will become apparent after I have discussed Rejewski's brilliant cryptanalytical work. Its name was given to it by Jerzy Rozycki because the idea for the machine came to Rejewski while the three of them were together and happened to be eating a very popular ice cream, known as a *bomba*, plural *bomby*.

II

THE CRITICAL SIX MONTHS: AUGUST 1939 TO JANUARY 1940

Towards the end of 1983 Andrew Hodges' fascinating book *Alan Turing – The Enigma*[12] reminded me of the early days at Bletchley Park, when Turing and I, with strong support from Edward Travis, then deputy head of GCHQ, were laying the foundations for Ultra. Until I read Hodges' book I did not know that Turing, while at Princeton before the war, had become interested in the use of machines for cryptanalysis. On his return to England he had made contact with Alastair Denniston's GC & CS and was working on Enigma with Dilly Knox, Peter Twinn and Tony Kendrick before the Poles revealed their secrets at Pyry.

The vital secret was the Enigma machine, of which the Poles gave us a replica. The Poles told Knox about the methodology that they had developed and the machines they had built, namely the bomba and the cyclometer. The most important method at that time had been invented by Zygalski and involved the use of large numbers of perforated sheets.

Although I have no firm information on what happened immediately after Pyry, it seems that Knox, Twinn and Kendrick must have set in motion the manufacture of perforated sheets early in August. Turing, probably in consultation with the others, developed several of the new ideas that were involved in the British bombe. Travis made arrangements for the manufacture of the bombe by British Tabulating Machine Company (BTM).

When I turned up at Bletchley at the outbreak of war in September 1939, I was sent along to join Dilly in the Cottage, but he soon sent me off to another building, the School, to work on call signs and discriminants. All I knew at this point was that the Poles had given us an Enigma machine, how it worked, and what enciphering procedures were then in use. I was not even told about the Zygalski sheets or about plans for the bombe. I knew nothing of the clever ways in which Rejewski, Zygalski and Rozycki had taken advantage of the weaknesses of earlier procedures.

As was explained in *The Hut Six Story*, my banishment from the Cottage to work on call signs and discriminants associated with intercepted Enigma messages proved extremely fortunate. In addition to masses of meaningless enciphered texts I was given a small number of decoded German Enigma messages. What happened then is summarised on pages 37 and 38 of my book as follows:

Previously I suppose I had absorbed the common view that cryptanalysis was a matter of dealing with individual messages, of solving intricate puzzles, and of working in a secluded backroom with little contact with the outside world. As I studied that first collection of decodes, however, I began to see, somewhat dimly, that I was involved in something very different. We were dealing with an entire communications system that would serve the needs of the German ground and air forces. The call signs came alive as representing elements of those forces, whose commanders at various echelons would have to send messages to each other. The use of different keys for different purposes, which was known to be the reason for the discriminants, suggested different command structures for the various aspects of military operations.

Much to the disgust of Dilly Knox I soon thought independently of the principle of the Zygalski sheets. Only then did I discover that the sheets were already being manufactured in the Cottage under the direction of John Jeffreys. I then realised that we were almost certainly going to be able to break a good deal of the Enigma traffic and also that, to exploit this great opportunity, we would need the well co-ordinated efforts of several specialised organisations, including the radio interception station at Chatham, with which I had already established close contact. We were faced with an unprecedented situation, quite unlike the cryptanalysts of the old days when messages were broken one by one. If we could discover a 'daily key' which told German operators how to set up their Enigmas, we would be able to decode all messages using that key. Each of several daily keys was valid for 24 hours, and even in the autumn of 1939, when no military operations were in progress, we were intercepting hundreds of messages each day.

No one else seemed to be doing anything about this potential gold mine, so I drew up a comprehensive plan which called for the close co-ordination of radio interception, analysis of intercepted messages, breaking Enigma keys by means of the perforated sheets, decoding messages on the broken keys, and extracting intelligence from the decodes. Travis immediately saw the urgent need to get moving. He won high-level approval for my plan and we were able to start recruiting the high-quality staff that would be needed.[13]

Even now, with all the interest that has been shown in its achievements, there is little if any recognition of the fact that, if Travis and I had not started the build-up of the Hut 6 organisation before the end of 1939, Ultra intelligence might never have come to bloom. For in May 1940, soon after Hitler invaded France, a simple change in enciphering procedure completely defeated the Polish method of using perforated sheets to break Enigma keys. By that time, fortunately, we had built up a strong team of young new-style cryptanalysts with the necessary supporting activities. They managed to hang on by their eyebrows, or rather by taking advantage of German errors, until the first British bombes arrived many months later.

This team, with its support, would not have been in place in May 1940 if we had not developed what was essentially a radically new production-oriented approach to machine cryptanalysis on a scale that Polish resources could not have achieved. Without the confident expectation and early demonstration of success we would not have been able to win high-level support for the major expansions of staff and facilities that were to prove so necessary. The early start on the manufacture of the Zygalski sheets, which, never having heard of Zygalski, I called the Jeffreys sheets, was of crucial importance to this early success. Furthermore, if the manufacture of the Turing bombe had not been started in August 1939, our early success would have fizzled out. Surprisingly these startling facts are not brought out in the official history of *British Intelligence in the Second World War*.

A good deal of importance has been attached to the fact that first the Poles and then the British brought in mathematicians to work on Enigma. Like Rejewski and Turing, I was a mathematician but, whereas they were both at home with deep problems of mathematical analysis, my principal interest lay in a descriptive approach to algebraic geometry, now out of fashion. However, soon after reinventing the Zygalski sheets, I came up with an abstract idea – the principle of the diagonal board – which greatly increased the power of the Turing bombe. My wartime associate, Pat Bayly,[14] maintains that this idea can be attributed to my pre-war habit of thinking in abstract multi-dimensional space.

III

THE FIRST TWO YEARS: AUGUST 1939–JULY 1941

We will be concerned with three of the many wooden huts that were built to house the activities of GCHQ, numbers 3, 6 and 8. The organisations that started in these huts were known throughout the war as Hut 3, Hut 6 and Hut 8, even after they all moved to a new brick building known as Block D.

Thanks to the flying start that the Poles gave us at Pyry and to the Bletchley Park initiatives of the first six months, we were able to build up a round-the-clock activity in Hut 6 that would support the breaks that were expected once the Jeffreys sheets became available.

For reasons that I will explain later I now believe that a set of the Jeffreys sheets was taken to the Poles at Bruno by Alan Turing on 17

January 1940, that Jeffreys moved from the Cottage to Hut 6 at about the same time, and that intermittent breaking started immediately both at Bletchley and at Bruno. Three members of the Foreign Office staff were assigned to handle the decodes and the intelligence organisation, Hut 3, came into existence.

When Hut 6 began to break with fair regularity, Commander Ellingworth, in charge of the intercept station at Chatham, was brought into the secret. He visited Hut 6, witnessed the breaking process, and talked to John Colman who was already operating our intercept control room round the clock. As a result of this visit the collaboration by telephone between Colman's duty officers and those at Chatham became firmly established. Incidentally the task of Colman's party was co-ordination rather than control, an important distinction.

At the start Jeffreys and his Machine Room handled the process of breaking, while I was concerned with the overall development and coordination of the necessary supporting activities. I did not become involved in the breaking until May 1940, when the sheets suddenly became useless. As will become apparent when I discuss Rejewski's work in part V, all the pre-war achievements of the Poles depended on the double encipherment of the wheel setting used to encipher and decipher the text of a message. Soon after they invaded France, the Germans abandoned this double encipherment. Hut 6 was on its own from then on.

We were saved from complete disaster by a form of operator carelessness known as Cillis and by an idea that had occurred to a new recruit, John Herivel, and had become known as the 'Herivel Tip'. The Cillis had been studied in the Cottage for some time. The form of operator laziness that provided the Herivel tip became sufficiently prevalent after the invasion of France, just when we needed it. The combination of these two German errors kept us in business and enabled us to study the decodes and be ready with cribs (accurate guesses at sections of clear text) when the bombes arrived many months later.[15]

Thanks to the success of the perforated sheets during their brief period of glory, the potential value of our ability to read Enigma traffic had been recognised. The Directors of Intelligence of the British army and the Royal Air Force had made it possible for the co-ordination of interception, traffic analysis, cryptanalysis and intelligence to be centralised at Bletchley Park. As I will endeavour to show in part VII, this was one of many things that really mattered.

The handling of naval intelligence derived from Enigma traffic of the German navy is another matter. Hut 8 was established to deal with naval Enigma, and Turing played a key role. But it was a tougher problem than that facing Hut 6. A capture was needed, and this was not achieved until March of 1941. I do not propose to say anything about this except to

THE BIRTH OF ULTRA

remark that the early success of Hut 6 won support for the development of the bombes on which the breaking of naval Enigmas would depend. The term 'Ultra', although originally coined by Winterbotham to describe intelligence derived from Hut 6 decodes, has been applied to information from other cryptanalytical sources, including Hut 8. For this reason I introduced the term 'Hut 6 Ultra'.

In September and October of 1940 we learned from Hut 6 decodes that Hitler had abandoned his plans for the invasion of England and that German forces were leaving France. It became clear that the area of operations of the German armies was going to spread into the Balkans and through Italy into Africa. This suggested that not only Hut 6 itself, but all its related activities as well, would need considerable expansion. Again I made a case to Travis and he got things moving. We got the additional capabilities that we needed for the crucial developments of March, April and May of 1941, when the Germans became active in the Balkans and in Africa. The RAF opened their big intercept station at Chicksands, a little to the east of Bletchley. The army station at Chatham moved to Beaumanor, a country estate in Leicestershire, some 50 miles north of Bletchley, where there was enough space for the large aerials needed to pull in distant radio signals.

Both Hut 6 and Hut 3 had begun a major expansion in the first half of 1941. Harold Fletcher, who arrived in August 1941 and was to be the principal administrator of Hut 6 and the bombes, found a well established organisation that was running smoothly. At that time we already had eight to twelve bombes. Thus, at the end of the second year, we had come a long way. The organisation that we had developed would stand up to the increasing complexity of our problems during the remaining four years of the war.

What had been achieved at Bletchley was to have many surprising ramifications. For example, in the second volume of *British Intelligence in the Second World War* Hinsley comments on the desert campaign from May to October 1942, from the lull before Rommel's attack at Gazala to his defeat in the second battle of El Alamein. It was thanks to Ultra, Hinsley says, that the importance of intelligence came to be recognised. At the start of the Gazala battles there was no adequate means of using Y intelligence, but this defect was spotted. Within two weeks, Army Y was fully integrated into the operational intelligence process at Eighth Army Headquarters. Thereafter it produced an extremely valuable flow of tactical intelligence about even the smaller enemy units. In the opinion of the British officer who was to become the head of Eighth Army's operational intelligence, Ultra put intelligence on the map in the Western Desert, but in battle the Army Y service was usually more valuable than Ultra.

Experience gained by the British intelligence community during the first two years was to have an effect on the war in the Pacific. As a result of his many personal contacts with Allied field commanders of the Second World War, Ronald Lewin in his *Ultra Goes to War*[16] stresses the importance of the 'Special Liaison Units' that were developed by Winterbotham to guide the use of Ultra intelligence in the field. The timely selection and training of officers for these units proved to be of the utmost importance. In his *American Magic*[17] Lewin remarks that, before the Japanese attack on Pearl Harbor on 7 December 1941, the Americans were ill-prepared for the problems of handling wartime intelligence, but in January 1942 Alfred McCormack of the New York Bar was assigned by Henry Stimson, the Secretary of War, to look into the matter. His early recommendations resulted in the birth of an intelligence organisation which, in its selection of personnel and its independent status was somewhat similar to Bletchley's Hut 3. Later, during a visit to Bletchley, McCormack was impressed by the well established organisation of SLUs. To build up a similar organisation of 'Special Branch Officers' he promptly recruited what he termed 'imaginative persons of first class ability', who would be attached to all major commands. Lewin's discussions with American field commanders showed that the value of these Special Branch Officers was well recognised everywhere except, apparently, by MacArthur.

Another event that was to be of importance to the Americans as well as to the British should be mentioned here. Before America entered the war, Alastair Denniston, who was head of Bletchley Park during the first two years, visited William Friedman, the chief cryptologist of the US army. One of Friedman's assistants, Frank Rowlett, who played a major role both in the breaking of the Japanese Magic Cipher machine and in the development of an American cipher machine, remembers the visit well. He and Friedman very much admired Denniston both as a person and as an outstanding cryptologist. Rowlett says that the impression Denniston made on the US Army's cryptological organisation undoubtedly helped to establish the close relations with Bletchley Park that were to develop later.

IV

CAUSES OF CONFUSION

Appendices B to E of Wladyslaw Kozaczuk's book, *Enigma*, are based on Marian Rejewski's own accounts of what happened in Poland before the war. These accounts are very clear, and they ring true. They are based on personal recollections that were written down in 1941 and 1942, when Rejewski's memory was still fresh. But few people have taken the trouble

THE BIRTH OF ULTRA 79

to understand them and as a result misconceptions have arisen. Too much attention has been paid to the statements of his superiors who, though making major contributions in other ways, were never in close contact with Rejewski's cryptanalytical work, which started in 1932.

The superiors were Colonel Stefan Mayer, chief of the intelligence department of the Polish General Staff, Colonel Gwido Langer, head of the Polish Cipher Bureau and Maksymilian Ciezki, head of the German section in the Cipher Bureau. According to Rejewski, Ciezki would come to see him once a day, Langer very seldom, and Mayer once or maybe twice during the whole period from 1932 to 1939.[18]

Kozaczuk's Appendix F, written by Christopher Kasparek and Richard Woytak, is entitled 'Polish and British Methods of Solving Enigma'. Referring to my book, *The Hut Six Story*, the first page contains the statement:

> It is disconcerting to find such a cock-and-bull story repeated with approval in Welchman's otherwise sober and valuable book when so much documentation regarding Polish mastery of Enigma has been published in English.

What seems to me 'disconcerting' is that Kasparek and Woytak, who should have been familiar with the 'documentation', arrived at such a misconception. They should have known that Rejewski's determination of the wiring of the two new wheels (the subject matter of the 'story') was the result of an extraordinary German error. As I said,[19] the article by Jean Stengers did not explain how the wiring became known to Rejewski. Nor did Lisicki's appendix to Garlinski's book *The Enigma War*, published in American in 1980. The true explanation was made known in two articles by Rejewski, first published in English in 1981 and 1982 and reissued as Appendices D and E of Kozaczuk's book, but these were not available to me until after my book went to press in mid-August 1981. I believe that any cryptanalyst who cares to study the matter will agree that a recovery of the wiring of the two new wheels by pure cryptanalysis (without a compromise or a major German blunder) was hard to believe and that it was logical for me to think that the Poles had probably pulled off a capture without the Germans knowing that they had done so.[20] Indeed this is exactly what the British did later on in order to break into the German naval Enigma.[21]

In a review for the *Journal of the U.S. Army War College*, Professor Cipher Deavours, Professor of Mathematics at Kean College, New Jersey, and an editor of *Cryptologia*, says that the Kozaczuk book contains valuable historical lessons for today and is well worth reading. He also says:

The book's chief flaw consists of its notably anti-British approach. In particular Welchman (whose book is quoted at excessive length) comes in for a lot of undeserved criticism. It is the thesis of the book that 'virtually all major cryptologic techniques that the British used to break Enigma in World War II had been thought of by the Poles earlier'. This statement is simply not true.

Without the Polish work, the British would likely never have gotten started in the first place, but once they did get started, British codebreaking was as dazzling as the earlier Polish accomplishments. The British bombes were in no way related to or derived from the earlier Polish bomby, nor were Polish methods of cryptanalysis particularly useful after the Germans changed to a better message keying system in May 1940.

In fairness I must say that Kozaczuk and his associates had good reason to be resentful of the way British authorities have belittled the Polish contributions to Allied success, on the battlefield as well as in the field of cryptanalysis. But it is unfortunate that they quoted so extensively from *The Hut Six Story* without any reference to me. This has added to the confusion because their Appendix F has repeated, and perhaps given additional credence to, many of my errors (as well as introducing many errors of their own).

To deal with the many misconceptions of Rejewski's brilliant work I will give a summary of what actually happened, based on Rejewski's own statements. Before I do that, however, it should be pointed out that a good deal of confusion has arisen because the relevant information has become available in dribs and drabs. (Some of it is still withheld by the British authorities.) This point is brought out in the chronological list of references at the end of this article. For example, Johnson's *The Secret War* and Hinsley's Appendix 1 to Volume 1 (references 11 and 15), both of which are full of mis-statements, were written before my book (reference 26) came out. Other authors, e.g. Lewin, Jones and Calvocoressi (references 9, 12 and 18) made fewer mistakes. I myself, having been told nothing by Dilly Knox and not having seen the Rejewski writings, was often reduced to guessing. I did try, however, to distinguish between my own direct experience and what seemed probable. My 'approval' of the 'cock-and-bull story' was the statement: 'I am inclined to believe that something of the sort must have occurred.'

Another major source of confusion is the different terminologies that have been used by the many authors who have written about Enigma. I will try to sort things out by comparing my terminology with that used by Rejewski. A good starting point is Figure 3.6 on page 50 of my book, which shows the electrical connections between lampboard, keyboard, steckerboard and scrambler of the German military Enigma. This gives a more detailed representation of the steckerboard than Rejewski's Figures D–4 and E–3.[22] Note that I use the term 'wheel', while Rejewski uses 'drum' in D–4 and 'rotor' in E–3. I use letters U, L, M, R to represent the four wheels (*Umkehrwaltze*, Left, Middle, Right) of what I call the scrambler unit. Rejewski uses letters R, L, M, N (R for Reversing) and replaces my in-out scrambler terminals by another drum or rotor, called H in D–4 and E (for Entry) in E–3. The two sides of a wheel, drum or rotor are shown in D–3.[23]

In comparing my Figure 3.6 with Rejewski's D–4 and E–3 we run immediately into an important difference of attitude. In all my work on Enigma I knew, because the Poles had told us, that the lower stecker terminals A, B, C, ... Z were connected to scrambler in-out terminals A, B, C, ... Z. This is represented in my diagram by a 26-way connector cable. It never occurred to me to worry about the possibility that the Germans might have introduced yet another permutation at this point. This possibility was very much in Rejewski's mind, and is allowed for in his diagrams by the entry rotor, E of his Figure E–3, shown as drum H in Figure D–4. Knox too had been very much concerned about this possibility.

A minor cause of confusion is that I reserve the word 'drum' to mean one of the rotating units in the double-ended scramblers of Doc Keen's engineering design of the British bombe.[24] There was no Polish equivalent.

Further confusion is caused by different usages of the words 'key' and 'setting'. The keyboard of an Enigma has keys, which I call 'letter keys' to distinguish them from machine keys. In my description of the Enigma,[25] I use the word 'key' to mean the basic set-up of the machine, consisting of the wheel order (*Walzenlage* in the German instruction manual), the settings of the alphabet rings on each wheel (*Ringstellung*) and the cross pluggings on the steckerboard, or 'stecker' (*Steckerverbindung*). Rejewski uses the term 'daily key', which I will adopt here.

At this point I can remove a cause of confusion by introducing the term 'crypto net' to mean a group of units who are issued with the same daily key so that they can communicate with each other. The German radio nets are something else.[26] A radio net could carry encrypted messages of several crypto nets, while a crypto net could use several radio nets. It is extraordinary that these two simple facts have been so little recognised.

So a daily key was issued to members of a crypto net. Discriminants (*Kenngruppen*) were used in the preambles of messages to indicate which crypto net was involved.

I used the term 'machine setting' to mean the positions of the three wheels in an Enigma Scrambler that is already set up in accordance with the daily key of a crypto net.[27] The encoding of an individual message involved two machine settings:

1. A 'text setting' at which encipherment would start
2. An 'indicator setting' (*Grundstellung*) used to encipher the text setting.

Rejewski calls the text setting a 'key', or 'message key'. He calls the indicator setting the 'basic position'. I will stick to my terminology here.

When I came into the picture in September 1939 I was told how the Germans were using their Enigma at that time. The daily keys for a month were issued to all units of a crypto net. Individual messages were enciphered at text settings chosen by the originating operator. These text settings were enciphered twice at an indicator setting also chosen by the operator. The indicator setting was transmitted in the preamble of the message, and the double enciphered indicator setting, which I called the 'indicator', was transmitted as the first six letters of the enciphered text. The receiving operator, with his machine set up to the same daily key would set his wheels to the indicator setting, decipher the indicator, and so obtain the text setting repeated twice. He would then set his wheels to this text setting and decipher the message.

Let me reiterate that Dilly Knox never told me about Rejewski's work, which I will describe in part V. I and the people who joined me in Hut 6 knew that the Poles had given us a replica of the Enigma, and we soon had modified Typex machines that operated like German military Enigma machines. We knew Zygalski's principle of perforated sheets. We knew the purpose of the discriminants and the way in which the units of a German crypto net would set up their Enigmas to a daily key. And we knew the indicating procedure used at that time for the encipherment and decipherment of individual messages. That was all! But it was enough. Knowledge of the other methods that had been used by the Poles would not have helped us. What really mattered was the machine itself and the stimulus that came from knowing that the Enigma traffic could be broken.

V

REJEWSKI'S BRILLIANT CRYPTANALYSIS

Six Successive Periods

At the end of his recent article Stengers remarks:

> What the Poles themselves did was the result, primarily, of Rejewski's creative spirit. But Rejewski himself could have remained impotent without the Asche documents, and the Asche

THE BIRTH OF ULTRA

documents were just a bit of luck. A bit of luck and history is changed.

In my chapter, 'A Comedy of Errors', I discuss the principal German errors that led to our success and the simple ways in which we could have been defeated. I concluded with the remark that 'We were lucky'.[28]

Rejewski and his two colleagues had different problems but similar luck. At one point[29] he remarks that a German slip-up (mixing plain text with code) made it possible to break into the Enigma traffic of the *Sicherheitsdienst* or SD, an achievement that, combined with another German error, led to the recovery of the wiring of wheels IV and V. He also remarks that the Germans would have been better off if they had not enciphered their text settings.

To get rid of misconceptions we must distinguish between the very different situations that existed in six successive periods, as follows:

1. From the turn of 1927/28 to September 1932, when Rejewski was assigned to work on Enigma.
2. The brief period from September 1932 to the turn of 1932/33 during which Rejewski, working in isolation, broke the German military Enigma.
3. The relatively quiet period from early 1933 to the end of 1935, during which Rejewski and his team achieved regular breaks of daily keys.
4. From 1 January 1936 to 15 September 1938, a period during which the work load increased, due in part to the introduction of new crypto nets for which daily keys had to be recovered.
5. The three months from 15 September 1938 to 15 December 1938 during which the Polish team were dealing with a major change in the German indicating procedure.
6. From the German introduction of two new wheels, IV and V, on 15 December 1938 to the Pyry disclosures to the French and British of July 1939.

1. Turn of 1927/28 to September 1932

The interest of the Polish Cipher Bureau in Enigma was aroused at the turn of 1927/28 when, on a Saturday afternoon, a package from the German Reich arrived at the Warsaw Customs Office. According to the accompanying declaration it contained radio equipment. The German firm's representative demanded very strenuously that the package be returned to the Reich even before going through Customs, since it had been shipped by mistake. The customs officials were suspicious and notified the Cipher Bureau, which was interested in new developments of radio equipment. The package could not be returned until after the weekend, so personnel from the Bureau had plenty of time to investigate. They carefully opened the box and found that it contained a cipher machine. They examined the machine minutely and carefully closed the box again.[30]

Rejewski insists that this Enigma was a commercial model with no steckerboard. The military model had not yet been put into use. Indeed the first machine-enciphered messages did not appear on German military radio nets until 18 July 1928. The importance of the incident lay in the fact that it revealed German interest in the Enigma. The Polish Cipher Bureau bought one of the commercial machines. At the turn of 1928/29 they organised a cryptology course in Poznan for mathematics students who were fluent in German. This proved to be good thinking.

2. September 1932 to the turn of 1932/33

The second period started on 1 September 1932 when three students who had attended this course, Rejewski, Zygalski and Rozyki, were hired to work permanently at the Cipher Bureau in Warsaw. Rejewski was soon separated from his two colleagues, given a separate room, and instructed to study Enigma. (Earlier studies had been abandoned.) The commercial machine was placed at his disposal, but was of no assistance. Each day he was given several dozen messages enciphered on the military machine.

At that time the German method of using their Enigma was very different from that with which Hut 6 was to be faced seven years later. Of the items in the daily key the wheel order was only changed once a quarter and only six pairs of letters were steckered, leaving 14 unsteckered. The indicator setting was specified as another item in the daily key. From 1 January 1936 the wheel order was changed once a month; from 1 October 1936 it was changed daily, and the number of stecker pairs, instead of being fixed at six, began to vary from five to eight. The indicator setting continued to be part of the daily key until 15 September 1938, after which date the indicator setting for each message was chosen by the operator. It was fortunate that Rejewski was set to work before these improvements in procedure were made.

The fact that the Germans continued for so long to use the same indicator setting for all messages on the same daily key, an extraordinary error, was brilliantly exploited by Rejewski. It became apparent to him that the first six letters of each message text, that I call the 'indicator',[31] were obtained by enciphering the three-letter text setting twice at the same indicator setting. In other words, for all messages on the same daily key the six-letter indicators were the result of encipherment at the same sequence of six positions of the Enigma.

Rejewski denotes the letter permutations produced by the Enigma in these six positions by A, B, C, D, E, F. He started by writing the six-letter

THE BIRTH OF ULTRA

indicators of all messages on a daily key underneath each other. All the indicators that had the same first letter also had the same fourth letter, obtained from the first by the product AD of permutations A and D. The same applied to the second and fifth, and to the third and sixth, involving the products BE and CF.

His next move was to have far-reaching results. Starting with any one of the indicators he wrote down the first letter, say d, and next to it the fourth, say v. He then sought out another indicator that had v as its first letter and wrote its fourth letter, say p, next to d and v. Thus, if three indicators were:

```
d m q v b n
v o n p u y
p u c f m g
```

he would obtain the sequence:

```
d v p f
```

continuing this process he would obtain a cycle of letters such as:

```
d v p f k x g z y o
```

which was closed by the fact that, if the first letter of an indicator was o, the fourth would be the starting letter d.

The remaining indicators would give further closed cycles of the permutation AD. The same procedure would be applied to BE and CF, giving three sets of cycles such as:

AD = (dvpfkxgzyo)(eijmunqlht)(bc)(vw)(a)(s)
BE = (blfqveoum)(hipswizrn)(axt)(cyg)(d)(k)
CF = (abvikrigfcqny)(duzrehlxwpsmo)

This simple method of representing the permutations AD, BE and CF, which Rejewski hit on right away, turned out to be of immense importance. He found that the composition of the cycles was different each day. Later on he would call the three sets of cycles the 'characteristics' of the permutations AD, BE and CF.

Rejewski quickly developed a mathematical theory of these characteristics and, by guessing that some German operators might select three identical letters, such as aaa, bbb, for their text settings, he was able to recover the six permutations A, B, C, D, E, F and so determine the text settings of all messages on the same daily key. In fact, without knowing either the internal connections of the wheels or the set up of a daily key, he had broken the indicating system. To form the three complete characteristics of a daily key all he needed was about 60 messages on that key. It sounds incredible, but it happened.

Still working in isolation, Rejewski's next step was to develop a mathematical representation of the working of the Enigma machine. He was hoping that the knowledge of permutations A to F would enable him to work out the wiring of the wheels. He had reduced his problem to a set of six equations involving three unknown permutations, and he was wondering whether they could be solved, when, on 9 December 1932, at just the right moment, he was given four documents. He did not know it at the time, but these documents had been obtained by Bertrand from the German traitor Asche.

The four documents were a *Gebrauchsanweisung* (operating instructions), a *Schlusselanleitung* (keying instructions), a table of daily keys for the month of September 1932, and a table of daily keys for the month of October 1932.

It was extremely fortunate that the two months, September and October, occurred in different quarters, during which different wheel orders were in use. The known daily keys for each month, combined with the equations he had developed, enabled him to work out the internal wiring of the two different wheels that appeared on the right. Finding the connections of the third wheel and the *umkehrwalze* presented him with no great difficulties. For each wheel he was able to determine the correct torsion of the sides with respect to each other and the turn-over positions of the alphabet rings. The establishment of all these details depended on attempts to read several messages. Fortunately each of the two monthly tables of daily keys included a sample plain text and its encipherment at a stated daily key and text setting.

At one point in this recovery process Rejewski had seemed to be near defeat. In formulating his equations he had assumed that the wiring of the entry wheel (equivalent to the connections of the 26-way cable in my Figure 3.6[32]) was known to him. At first he assumed that the connections were the same as those of the commercial Enigma, in which the terminals of the scrambler's input-output ring were connected to the terminals of the keyboard and lamps in the order in which letters appeared on the keyboard, namely:

q w e r t z u i o a s d f g h j k p y x c v b n m l

This assumption, being wrong, was getting him nowhere, when, at the end of December 1932, or perhaps in the first days of January 1933, he wondered whether the Germans might have used the alphabetical sequence a b c ... z instead of the keyboard sequence q w e ... l. This inspired guess proved correct. The very first trial yielded a positive result. Then, from his pencil, as if by magic, began to issue numbers designating the connections of the right-hand wheel.[33]

Now that the wiring was known, the Poles could modify their commercial Enigma to operate like the German military Enigma. At this point Rejewski was allowed to initiate Zygalski and Rozycki so that, using the daily keys supplied by Bertrand, they could decipher messages that had been intercepted during September and October 1932. Rejewski continued to work in isolation on the third part of his task. He had broken the system of enciphering text settings. He had worked out the electrical and mechanical details of the military Enigma. He still had to find a means of recovering daily keys, and this, as he modestly says, was 'hardly easy'. He developed what he called the 'grill' method. It was very laborious, but, combined with the fact, shown up by decodes of September and October 1932, that many plain texts began with the three letters A N X, it was effective. Thus in January 1933 the Poles were in business. They were able to decode current Enigma traffic. What an extraordinary achievement for a period of a little over four months! And what a brilliant one-man triumph for Rejewski!

3. *Early 1933 to the end of 1935*

When Rejewski reported his success, the Cipher Bureau ordered a series of replicas of the German military Enigma to be built. (Rejewski calls them 'doubles'.) Then five or six young persons were hired to decipher intercepted messages, the keys to which were soon forthcoming. Zygalski and Rozycki were assigned to work permanently with Rejewski.

Day by day the daily keys were recovered by this three-man team. For three years, until the end of 1935, the Germans introduced no essential changes, so time could be devoted to improving methodology. In his mathematical representation Rejewski had used letter Q to denote the permutation produced by the middle wheel, left-hand wheel and *umkehrwaltze*. A catalogue was made of all the possible permutations Q so that, when the early stages of the grill method had determined the setting of the right hand wheel and the permutation Q, reference to the catalogue would at once reveal the settings of the other two wheels. Rozycki worked out a 'clock method' which, in many cases, could determine which wheel was on the right. This became important when changes of wheel order occurred monthly, and then daily, instead of quarterly. At some point German operators were forbidden to use text settings consisting of three identical letters, but they developed other habits which still allowed the Polish team to determine the permutations A to F.

4. *1 January 1936 to 15 September 1938*

The fourth period saw two very important developments; the invention of the Cyclometer and the breaking of the SD Enigma traffic. Already, from 1 August 1935, the German air force had created its own crypto net with its own daily keys. Gradually other military and paramilitary organisations joined in, forming additional crypto nets with their own daily keys. This implied a great increase in the work load of the three-man team. Furthermore, from 1 October 1936, five to eight pairs of stecker were used, which made it difficult to apply Rejewski's grill method. It became necessary to look for other methods.

Thoughts went back to the characteristics that Rejewski had investigated in September 1932. It dawned on the team that, if they could make a complete catalogue of all possible characteristics, the recovery of the three characteristics of a new daily key, achieved as usual by an analysis of indicators, would lead very quickly to the complete recovery of that daily key. The time-consuming demands of the grill method would be avoided.

Rejewski then invented a machine, the Cyclometer, that would permit the construction of this catalogue. It consisted of two Enigma scramblers with the right-hand wheel of the second scrambler displaced three positions with respect to that of the first scrambler. The overall layout is shown in his Figure E–4, the interconnections of the two scramblers in Figure E–5.[34] The cycles of a characteristic always occurred in complementary pairs of equal length. When current was turned on at any letter, all letters in the same cycle and in the complementary cycle would be shown up by lamps.

This is shown in Figure E–5, in which the 'reversing drum' represents the permutation Q, which is assumed to remain unchanged. When a switch puts current into the first (left-hand) scrambler at position 1, it returns at position r, enters the second scrambler at this position and returns at position w and, after going through the second scrambler unit again, returns to the starting position 1. Thus, for the particular setting of the wheels that is being tested, we have two complementary cycles (l,z) and (r,w). Using other switches reveals the other pairs of complementary cycles. The cyclometer had a rheostat because the number of lamps to be lit would vary.

In September 1932 Rejewski obtained three characteristics for the permutations AD, BE and CF involved in the double encipherment of text settings. Now, for each of the six wheel orders and each of the $26 \times 26 \times 26$ possible positions of the first scrambler, the cyclometer would enable him to obtain a characteristic. The cycle lengths of each characteristic would be entered on a card, probably in order of decreasing magnitude, and the $6 \times 26 \times 26 \times 26$ cards so obtained would be arranged as a card index. Once this major task was accomplished, the recovery of a new daily key would be greatly simplified. The first step, as before, would be to accumulate enough intercepted messages on a new daily key to permit the construction of the characteristics of the three permutations AD, BE and CF. These three characteristics would be looked up in the

THE BIRTH OF ULTRA 89

card index and, as a rule, the break would be completed in 10–20 minutes.[35]

Rejewski does not say how the turn-over problem was handled, but, except in the worst possible case, at least one of the permutations AD, BE, CF would be unaffected by turn-over and this would greatly reduce the labour involved in completing the break.

The Polish team had a severe setback when on 2 November 1937, soon after the card catalogue of characteristics had been completed, the Germans introduced a new *umkehrwaltze*. At about the same time, however, luck smiled on them once again.

In September 1937 a new crypto net had appeared. It was used by the *Sicherheitsdienst*, or SD. The usual methods provided the wheel order, indicator setting and stecker but attempts to complete a break by looking for messages that began with the letters A N X failed. The ring settings could not be determined. This problem arose from the use of a four-letter code to represent the clear text before it was enciphered on the Enigma. But the Germans enciphered the word '*ein*', for which it seems that there was no four-letter code. With perhaps one and a half ounces of luck this was spotted. The Polish team proceeded to break the four-letter code, and the breaking of the SD crypto net became routine.

5. *The three months 15 September 1938 to 15 December 1938*

The change of *umkehrwaltze* on 2 November 1937 was nothing compared with the blow that hit the Polish team in September 1938. Every single technique that they had used until then had depended on the inexplicable German error of using the same indicator setting for the double encipherment of the text settings of all messages using the same daily key. Suddenly, on 15 September 1938, new regulations called for the arbitrary selection by each operator of the indicator setting for each message. The doubly enciphered text setting – the indicator – still appeared as the first six letters of the enciphered text. The chosen indicator setting was included in the preamble.

The response of the Polish team to this change was amazingly rapid. Within a few weeks – Rejewski estimates one or two – they developed ways to realise two new ideas. Furthermore – and this was a real stroke of luck – they could still read traffic on the SD crypto net which had not yet applied the new procedure.

There were two inventions – the 'bomba' by Rejewski and the 'perforated sheets' by Zygalski. Of these the bomba was a development from the cyclometer, which grew out of Rejewski's very early discovery of the characteristics. Its importance has been greatly exaggerated.

Thinking about the characteristics now became focused on whether or not a characteristic contained a pair of single-letter cycles. In the example that I have quoted from Rejewski, the characteristics of AD and BE do, whereas that of CF does not. When the characteristic of AD does contain single-letter cycles, it is possible for the same letter to turn up in the first and fourth positions of an indicator. Otherwise it is impossible for this to happen. Similarly for BE and CF.

Until I read the Rejewski papers I thought that the term 'female' for an indicator in which the first and fourth, or the second and fifth, or the third and sixth letters were the same, had been introduced at Bletchley Park. It now seems that an equivalent term was introduced by the Poles. I also thought that Turing's ideas for a British bombe must have been based on what he had learned of the Polish bomba. Again I was wrong, because I had no knowledge of what the bomba was designed to do. It is strange that Kasparek and Woytak, with all the evidence available to them, should have endorsed this mistake of mine in Appendix F of Kozaczuk's book.

When the Germans made their operators responsible for selecting the indicator setting for each message, the Poles were no longer able to recover the characteristics, but, for each message with its chosen indicator setting, the occurrence of a female in the indicator would indicate that the corresponding permutation, AD, BE or CF, had a characteristic that contained single-letter cycles. This was the basis of both inventions.

Rejewski says:[36]

> Given sufficiently ample cipher material it may happen that on a given day there will be three messages with keys (indicator settings and indicators in my terminology) such as:
>
> | R T J | W A H | W I K |
> | H P L | R A W | K T W |
> | D Q X | D W J | M W R |

The bomba depended on the assumption that the letter W was unsteckered. It required little engineering development because it was essentially three cyclometers, set to the relative positions at which the females had occurred, and then turned automatically (as opposed to manually in the generation of the catalogue of characteristics) through all possible positions.[37] In each position there would be a simple automatic test of whether (assuming letter W to be unsteckered) the three females could have occurred. Six bomby were quickly built, one for each of the six possible wheel orders. Rejewski says that they worked reasonably well as long as the number of stecker pairs varied from 5 to 8. From 1 January 1939 this number was increased to 7 to 10, and the bomby became ineffective. By the time the British became involved the number of stecker pairs had settled at ten. Thus the idea that the British would have wanted to copy the bomba is sheer nonsense.

THE BIRTH OF ULTRA

Zygalski's invention of a method based on perforated sheets was a different matter.[38] It involved no assumptions that certain letters would be unsteckered, and it was immediately copied by the British after Pyry. Because the indicator setting was now chosen by the operator for each message, the characteristics AD, BE and CF would no longer apply to all messages on the same daily key. It would no longer be possible to recover them. On the other hand the occurrence of a female such as:

    K I E   S̲ P E   S̲ N T   (a 1–4 female)

would mean that the AD characteristic associated with the indicator setting K I E must contain a pair of single-letter cycles. The same would apply to the BE and CF characteristics of females such as:

    R Y M   X W̲ N   P W V   (a 2–5 female)
    L T S   V B Y̲   Q G Y̲   (a 3–6 female)

What was needed, therefore, for each wheel order, was a catalogue of indicator settings, whose characteristics contain single-letter cycles, and a means of comparing females appearing on the same daily key with this catalogue. It was found that about 40 per cent of the characteristics, shown up by the cyclometer and recorded in the card index, contained single-letter cycles, and Zygalski found a way of making the comparison.

For each of the six possible wheel orders a paper sheet was used to represent each of the 26 possible positions of the left-hand wheel. On each sheet a large rectangle was divided into 51 × 51 small rectangles. The two sides, the top, and the bottom of the large rectangle were lettered 'a' to 'z', and again 'a' to 'y'. This provided a co-ordinate system in which the little rectangles corresponded to positions of the middle and right-hand wheels. In each small rectangle a hole would be perforated if the characteristic of the corresponding setting of the three wheels contained a single-letter cycle. Each such occurrence would call for as many as four perforations.

Given enough females on the same daily key, it was possible to stack sheets on top of each other in accordance with the indicator settings that had given rise to the females. The number of visible apertures would steadily decrease and any left open would represent ring settings that would permit the females to occur.[39] Note that, because the turn-over notches were on the alphabet rings, it would be known whether a turnover of the middle wheel would occur between the encipherments of the two identical letters. Consequently any female that would involve a turnover could be discarded.

It is perhaps of interest to note that, when I thought of the same idea, independently, I knew nothing of Rejewski's characteristics. In my attempted reconstruction of my thinking process at the beginning of my

Chapter 4, I realised, as Step 3, that it was not always possible for the Enigma to produce the same letter pairing in two positions three places apart in its cycle. This is equivalent to saying that a characteristic will not always contain a pair of single-letter cycles. From then on my thinking was probably very similar to Zygalski's.

Rejewski and his team had to do the enormous job of cutting about a thousand apertures in each sheet, and they cut them with razor blades! They needed six series of 26 sheets each for the six possible wheel orders and the 26 possible positions of the left-hand wheel. By 15 December 1938 they had made only two series. On that day the Germans started using two new wheels IV and V, which had been issued to all formations, including the SD.[40] This meant 60 possible wheel orders, calling for 60 series of perforated sheets.

6. *15 December 1938 to July 1939*

The quick recovery of the wiring of the two new wheels by cryptanalysis – the achievement that I found hard to believe – was made possible by yet another major German error. The SD crypto net introduced the two new wheels on the appointed date, but it was still using the old system of enciphering text settings, which had been abandoned by all other crypto nets on 15 September 1938. Knowing this, the team found a day on which the right hand wheel was on of the original three and applied Rejewski's original grill method. Then, assuming that the left-hand and middle wheels were a known one and an unknown one, they found the connections of the latter wheel in the same way that Rejewski had found the wiring of the wheel that had not appeared on the right in September or October 1932.

Knowing the wiring of all five wheels, the Poles, still a three-man team, continued to read messages of the SD crypto net.[41] This reading was intermittent because although Rozycki's clock method sometimes revealed which wheel was on the right, the grill method – the only method of breaking still applicable – sometimes failed because from 1 January 1939 the number of stecker pairs had risen from seven to 10.

This increase in the number of stecker pairs would have reduced the effectiveness of the bomba, and in any case limited Polish resources prohibited the construction of 54 new bomby to deal with the additional wheel orders. The preparation of 58 more series of perforated sheets was another virtually insoluble problem. It was only possible to read military messages when the three original wheels happened to be in use in the two combinations covered by the existing perforated sheets. When, on 1 July 1939, the SD crypto net shifted to the new indicating procedure, the old grill method ceased to be effective there too.

This was the situation in July 1939, when the Poles told Alastair

Denniston and Dilly Knox all they knew. What I knew of what happened after my arrival at Bletchley Park at the outbreak of war is outlined in *The Hut Six Story*. I still feel very strongly, as a result of some 20 years of research on today's military problems, that this story contains many valuable lessons that are sadly neglected. But my account has two serious gaps. I still do not know what Dilly Knox achieved before Pyry, or what he was up to in August 1939, assisted by Twinn, Kendrick, Turing, and a few other assistants. Nor have I found it easy to obtain reliable information about the wartime collaboration between Dilly Knox and Rejewski's team when they were operating first at Bruno, near Paris, and later, under the code-name Cadiz, near the coast of Vichy, France. From what I have now learned from Polish writings, it seems to me that the achievements of the brilliant Dilly Knox have been belittled in his own country. Even if his cryptanalytical methods of around 45 years ago still need to be concealed, which I doubt, it seems strange that a broad outline of what he actually achieved, and might well have achieved with a little luck, is still subject to veto by today's Government Communications Headquarters.

VI

DILLY KNOX AND BRUNO

Marian Rejewski formed a very high opinion of Dilly Knox at the meeting in Pyry in July 1939. In a conversation with Woytak he said:

> Just how much Braquenie understood, I don't know; but there is no question that Knox grasped everything very quickly, almost as quick as lightning. It was evident that the British really had been working on Enigma. So they didn't require many explanations. They were specialists of a different kind.[42]

Rejewski also said:

> I have the fullest grounds to believe that the British cryptologists were unable to overcome the difficulties caused by the connections in the entry drum. When the meeting of Polish, French and British cipher bureau representatives took place in July 1939, the first question that the cryptologist Dilwyn Knox asked was: What are the connections in the entry drum?[43]

Like all the statements that Rejewski made from his own personal experience, these two ring true. And they make one wonder whether Dilly had actually thought of all the major Polish ideas and had been held up only by failing to make Rejewski's guess that the permutation of the entry drum might be identity.

It seems to me entirely possible that Dilly went through much the same thought processes as Rejewski and his team. He could certainly have discovered the characteristics, just as Rejewski did, and he could have gone on to break the indicator system. It is said that Bertrand brought some of the Asche documents to England, so Dilly may have received the four that were so helpful to Rejewski. In that case he could have been well on the way to recovering the wheel wirings, but prevented from doing so only by failure to guess the wiring of the entry drum. After the Germans stopped using the same indicator setting for all messages on the same daily key, it is possible that Dilly would have thought of Zygalski's idea of using perforated sheets to provide a catalogue of wheel settings that could produce females. After all, I had the same idea myself, and I had no previous experience of cryptanalysis.

Having female indicators on his mind, Dilly could well have thought of associating two Enigma scramblers set three positions apart, as was done in Rejewski's cyclometer. With Turing around it is quite possible that, before the Pyry conference the idea of mechanising the movement of the two scramblers would have emerged. The Polish bomba was essentially a combination of three mechanised cyclometers, and the idea of driving a set of scramblers automatically through all possible positions is the only feature of the Polish bomba that was used in the British bombe. It is even conceivable that, before Pyry, Turing and Dilly may have begun to think of using a larger battery of scramblers, not just to handle three females with the assumption that the letter involved would be self-steckered but to handle textual cribs with no such assumption. But, of course, the ideas of the perforated sheets and the battery of automatically driven scramblers could not be exploited without a knowledge of the wiring of the Enigma wheels, which was provided by the Poles at Pyry.

The development of the British bombe involved four new ideas, descriptions of which will be found in *The Hut Six Story*:

1. Loops derived from a crib (p. 79)
2. The double-ended Enigma scrambler (p. 297)
3. The diagonal board (p. 304)
4. Taking advantage of the 'filling up' of the test-register (p. 301)

In addition the design engineer, Doc Keen, used what I call 'drums' instead of wheels to get greater speed.[44] Lisicki has confirmed that none of these ideas were known to Rejewski. In a letter to me Lisicki said:

> None of the ideas which you listed were Rejewski's. He was happy with the sheets and discarded the idea of improving his bomba. The loops, the double-ended Enigma, the diagonal board, and the filling up of the test register were all British ideas, and Rejewski in his

letters to me several times mentioned that he had no idea how to mechanize the search for the keys and thought that the British mechanized the sheets, but that would be useless after May 1940. In Bruno he had absolutely no time for creative work. The running of a number of Enigma scramblers was the only idea which the Poles first used and perhaps was born from the Cyklometer.

My suggestions of what Knox may have done before Pyry are pure conjecture, based on Rejewski's feeling that he must have done a lot. Kozaczuk and Kasparek had no right to assert, as they appear to do, that none of the Polish ideas had been thought of by the British. Furthermore, as Deavours says in the review of the Kozaczuk book that I have quoted, their thesis that 'virtually all major cryptologic techniques that the British used to break Enigma in World War II had been thought of and used by the Poles earlier' is simply not true.

On the other hand the Poles did give us the wirings of the Enigma wheels, and I still maintain that, had they not done so, British breaking of the Enigma might well have failed to get off the ground. Indeed, it is deplorable that the official history of *British Intelligence in the Second World War* has tried to establish that the Polish contribution had little effect. More about this in the next section.

One would like to know how far Dilly had got with his Enigma studies before Pyry, what he did between Pyry and the outbreak of war, and also what he achieved in the Cottage up to his death in February 1943. It is public knowledge that his organisation, ISK (Intelligence Services Knox), broke an Italian naval cipher system and an Abwehr system both of which used Enigmas different from the German military version. He was probably in touch with Turing's work on naval Enigma. But at the moment I am concerned with matters relating to Huts 6 and 3, and I have found it very hard to determine what Dilly was doing while Hut 6 was getting established. This is no doubt partly due to Bletchley's wartime policy that individuals should know only what they needed to know, but also to Dilly himself. Babbage, who joined Knox around Christmas 1939, has said in a recent letter to me:

> I gradually got to understand the Enigma machine and the problems it posed, but this was mainly through people like Twinn and Kendrick. Dilly was a most entertaining person, but definitely *not* very informative, as you found.

Indeed, it is probable that even Twinn and Kendrick were not fully aware of what Dilly was up to. It is certain that, when I was banished from the Cottage to work in the School, Dilly had told me nothing at all about Pyry, about the perforated sheets that were already being punched, or about Enigma breaks that had been attempted in the Cottage. Nor was I told about the collaboration with Rejewski's team at Bertrand's Bruno, which seems to have been established in November 1939, when Travis and I were setting in motion the build-up of Hut 6. I am inclined to think, but have no supporting evidence, that this collaboration was handled by Dilly himself, or by ISK if it existed at that time, and that he was, as usual, '*not* very informative'.

In trying to sort out the sequence of events, I have come to believe that Turing took a complete set of the perforated sheets that Jeffreys produced to Bruno on 17 January 1940 and spent a few days with Rejewski and his team. The anecdotes that Rejewski relates about the farewell supper given before Turing returned to England are convincing.[45] For example, Zygalski wondered why each little square in the British version of his perforated sheets had so peculiar a measurement — about eight and a half millimetres on a side. 'That's perfectly obvious', said Turing, laughing. 'It's simply one third of an inch.'

From my memory I would have guessed a later date for the availability of the Jeffreys sheets in Hut 6, but John Herivel's arrival fits in with the 17 January date. He arrived at Bletchley Park on 29 January 1940 and went straight to Hut 6, where Jeffreys and his sheets were already installed. We cannot have been having much success with the sheets at that time, because, once he had got the hang of the machine, Herivel found himself continually wondering how to find a way to break into it. Then, one evening in early February, at his digs, he had the idea of the Herivel tip, or Herivelismus as Kendrick used to call it. He remembers that, when he related his idea to colleagues the following day, it was immediately recognised as a possible way into the Enigma. He thinks that the idea of looking for clusters on a 'Herivel Square' came from me,[46] but I have always thought it was his own. He believes that nothing significant was observed until the German blitzkrieg of May 1940, when suddenly a number of Enigma operators were careless and the 'neighbourhood' of the ring settings for the day stood out clearly on a Herivel Square. This was providential, in view of the fact that the perforated sheets had suddenly become useless.

I myself had nothing to do with the actual breaking of daily keys until the crisis of May 1940, so it is not surprising that, when I was writing my book from memory, I thought that both the Herivel tip and what I mistakenly called 'sillies' were new ideas that occurred to us at that time. Actually the idea of Cillis had been worked on in the Cottage. It is even conceivable that Dilly was aware of them before Pyry. One would like to know. There were a lot of activities in the Cottage of which I was told nothing, as was brought to my attention by Polish accounts of Bruno.

A record was kept at Bruno of all keys broken and exchanged between

THE BIRTH OF ULTRA

B.P. and Bruno from 17 January 1940 to 21 June 1940. What may be deduced from this record is discussed in section VIII. The first Polish break of wartime Enigma came immediately after Turing delivered the Jeffreys sheets, and it seems that Hut 6 started breaking at about the same time. But, in view of Rejewski's impression at Pyry, it is by no means obvious that Dilly and his team did not achieve breaks at a much earlier date. Again one would like to know.

It seems a great shame that the accomplishments of a man who did so much for his country, and indeed for the world, have not been made known. He did outstanding work in Room 40 in the First World War, and stayed on with Alastair Denniston. Around 1936 he was tempted to return to academic life at King's College, Cambridge, but chose to continue his work on Enigma. Not very much is known of his successes with the Enigma machines that were used in the Spanish Civil War. And hardly anything is known of his achievements after that. Of the men who were closely associated with Dilly, both before and after Pyry, the only one alive is Peter Twinn. One would have thought that he would have been encouraged to write about Dilly, but he has been refused permission to do so. One would have thought, also, that the major achievements of other old-timers of GC & CS, such as Oliver Strachey, Josh Cooper, John Tiltman and Hugh Foss, would have been made public by now. Indeed the attitude of the British authorities to the people to whom so much was owed, British as well as Polish, is hard to understand, let alone justify.

Two stories involving Dilly Knox are worth mentioning. Just after the Warsaw–Pyry conferences of 24 and 25 July 1939, Dilly wrote a thank-you note to Rejewski, Zygalski and Rozycki saying, in Polish, 'My sincere thanks for your co-operation and patience'. He enclosed for each of them a set of little paper 'batons', inscribed with the letters of the alphabet.[47] Rejewski's comment was 'I don't know how Knox's method was supposed to work. Most likely he had hoped to vanquish Enigma'. Deavours, who published an article on the method of batons in *Cryptologia* of October 1980, believes that Dilly had actually used batons to break the commercial Enigma during the Spanish Civil War, but has been unable to confirm this.

The other story, as yet unexplained, concerns what was known to the Poles at Bruno and Cadiz as 'The Knox Method'. Lisicki tells me that this involved the Meteo Code, the Herivel tip, and a method of using operator carelessness to determine wheel order. The Meteo Code was a three-letter code used by the Germans for communicating weather information between an airfield and aircraft in flight. It first appeared at the turn of 1939/40, but apparently was not considered worth bothering about until around the time of the invasion of Norway, in April 1940. It was found that a reciprocal permutation was being applied to the letters of each code group in a message. Then the astonishing discovery was made that this permutation was the stecker permutation of the military Enigma key for the day.

Thus the first step of the 'Knox Method' was to break the Meteo Code for each day, which was not difficult. The next step was to use the Herivel tip, which began to perform well in May 1940, according to Herivel's memory. The third step was to determine the wheel order by an analysis of indicator settings and indicators that was different from the Cilli approach. The rest was easy.

This story of a method that Dilly seems to have made known to the Poles but not to Hut 6 is, I believe, only one of many instances in which Dilly generated ideas and did things without telling people who could have used the information. It would be interesting, for example, to know what Dilly did with the daily keys recovered by the Poles and sent to B.P. from Bruno. These keys could have been valuable in the catalogue of broken keys that was kept in Hut 6 by Reg Parker.[48] Knowledge that the Poles were breaking Green traffic would certainly have been of value to me, but it was not communicated.

It seems, in fact, that even if Peter Twinn is allowed to write an account of Dilly's activities before and during the war, there will be parts of the story that can never be told.

VII

THE BOMBE WAS NOT ALL THAT MATTERED

On page 184 of his official history of *British Intelligence in the Second World War* Hinsley states that the first bombe arrived in August 1940. This I can believe, though from memory I would have guessed September. On page 494 of his Appendix Hinsley changes the time of arrival to the end of May 1940 and goes on to say that 'it is possible to arrive at an actual measure of the Polish contribution to the successes against the wartime Enigma'. His argument leads to the conclusion that, in the absence of Polish assistance, the first bombe would have been delivered in January 1941 instead of in May 1940. This, in my opinion is utter nonsense. Furthermore, as I will attempt to show, the bombe was not all that mattered.

The January 1982 edition of *Cryptologia* ontained Rejewski's remarks, dated 2 December 1979, on Hinsley's Appendix 1, a copy of which had been sent to him by Woytak. In comments on 34 of Hinsley's statements, Rejewski shows that the Appendix gives a very inaccurate account of the Polish work. Hinsley is also misleading in his discussion of the British effort. His greatest error, in my view, is his complete failure to grasp the importance of the people who were involved.

It was extremely important that we were able to recruit enough high-quality people in time to take advantage of the opportunities that came our way. Hinsley was not at Bletchley in the early days and may not have been told of the sheer piracy that we were able to employ in our recruiting until the spring of 1941, when C.P. Snow was put in charge of the allocation of all scientists and mathematicians. Thanks to the Poles we got started quickly and recruited enough key people to see us through the crisis of May 1940. The success of this first round of recruits made it possible to go on recruiting for the expansion of our problems that lay ahead. Without assistance from the Poles, our recruitment of high-quality people would have been too little and too late.

To be more specific, if the Poles had not given us the details of the Enigma at Pyry, the British GC & CS would probably have continued to think that the Enigma problem was hopeless without a capture. Even if Turing had thought of his bombe, there would have been little or no justification for its engineering development. I would probably not have been assigned to work on Enigma, and who else would have thought of the diagonal board? The need for a production-oriented organisation would not have been apparent. If Herivel had not been recruited in January 1940, who would have thought of the Herivel tip, without which we would have been defeated in May 1940 – unable to maintain continuity until the bombes began to arrive many months later?

Let there be no misconceptions about this last point. Loss of continuity would, at all stages, have been very serious, if not disastrous. I feel confident in making this statement, even though I myself knew very little about how the Hut 6 team of 'wizards' dealt with their cryptanalytical problems. I can claim to have made their recruitment possible, early enough and in sufficient numbers. They did the job.

Hinsley was not the only one to concentrate far too much on the bombe. Another, as I have learned only recently, was Oscar Oeser, who was appointed in 1942 to be the spokesman for Hut 3 in matters of priority. In March of 1983 Jean Alington (now Mrs Jean Howard), who had been Oeser's deputy, was asked by the BBC to prepare a statement on the preparations that were made at Bletchley for D–Day. A year later, after talking to a lot of people who had been involved, she submitted a statement[49] and sent me a copy thinking it would be of interest. It certainly was.

What Jean had found most extraordinary about her research was how *little* everyone knew about the whole picture. For instance no one appeared to remember the large log-reading group that had been built up by M18, or the means by which interception had been co-ordinated with Hut 6 activities from the very beginning. She remarked: 'Each individual, working flat out, thought that they knew everything. In fact each individual had tunnel vision.' What happened, I think, is that people who arrived in Hut 3 after the first two years were put into slots in a well established organisation. Their assigned tasks kept them working flat out and, as Jean says, they did develop tunnel vision.

Jean herself arrived early enough to take part in the formative period in Hut 3. The Air Index, which was to prove of enormous importance, had been set up by Squadron Leader Reggie Cullingham in early 1941. Jean joined him in May 1941, at which time the whole index was contained in one shoebox. Oeser, then a Flight Lieutenant, was already one of the RAF representatives in Hut 3, which was then headed by Commander Saunders. The index, compiled from Hut 6 decodes, soon became a means of indoctrinating new arrivals in Hut 3. Jean remembers indoctrinating Peter Calvocoressi when he arrived early in 1942. Of the authors who have written about Ultra, Calvocoressi, in his *Top Secret Ultra*,[50] seems to me to have the best appreciation of the importance both of interception and of the overall co-ordination achieved by Hut 6 in the early days and maintained throughout the war.

During 1942, just as I was feeling the need for a much closer inter-relationship between Hut 6 and Hut 3, the organisation of Hut 3 was changing. Travis asked Saunders to focus his efforts on the obvious need for a greatly expanded bombe programme. Group Captain Jones came in to direct the equally obviously needed expansion of Hut 3. At my request he appointed Oeser, now a Wing Commander, as the spokesman for Hut 3 on matters of priority between our two organisations. When, in 1943, Oeser set up an organisation known as 3L, Jean joined him, leaving the Air Index activity which had grown to six girls on each shift.

I had hoped that Oscar would grasp the whole picture of what really mattered, making it known to key people in both Huts. But it now appears, from what Jean tells me, that this did not happen. He concentrated on bombe time and decoding, for which he developed 'coefficients of importance and urgency'. He himself was often away, leaving the donkey work of the bombe time exercise to Jean and his other assistants. He took little or no interest in the overall picture, and he did little to inform key people in Hut 3 of what was going on elsewhere. This is evidenced by the fact that, at an Anglo/Yugoslav Symposium at the Imperial War College, Jean heard Ralph Bennett, who had been a Hut 3 Duty Officer, state blandly: 'I suppose we just covered frequencies by luck.' She blew her top!

Fortunately the management of interception was in the hands of well qualified people, Commander Ellingworth and Wing Commander Shepherd. When I started to analyse Enigma messages in 1939, I established a close working relationship with Ellingworth at Chatham. At the turn of 1939/40 Hut 6 already had a 24-hour team under Colman, which kept in continual telephone contact with Ellingworth's duty officers.

THE BIRTH OF ULTRA

When, in 1941, the big RAF intercept station at Chicksands was opened, Wing Commander Shepherd co-operated closely with Ellingworth and Colman. Very soon Colman's team was working just as smoothly with the Duty Officers at Chicksands as they were with those of Ellingworth, who had moved his main station to Beaumanor. The organisation that was established in the first two years worked remarkably smoothly for the rest of the war.

The interception and analysis of radio nets carrying messages enciphered on the German military Enigma was not as simple a matter as it has been made out to be. The term 'frequency' as used by Bennett and others is misleading, for the radio sets of those days would drift badly. Each controller of a German radio net would have to struggle to maintain contact with and among his outstations, using chit-chat for this purpose.[51] Each of our intercept operators, struggling to keep in touch with the stations of a radio net, would be continually tuning to pick up the chit-chat. It would have been useless to tell our operators to keep their sets tuned to specified radio frequencies. On the other hand our experienced operators could identify individual German operators by their habits, even when their transmitters had drifted quite badly from assigned frequencies.

The analysis of the radio transmissions started with the intercept operator, who recorded all chit-chat and identifications on sheets of a 'log'. When the German net controller had paved the way for the transmission of an Enigma message, this message would be recorded on a separate sheet. The log sheets would go to the M18 log-reading group, which started in London and moved first to Harpenden, then to Beaumanor, and finally to Bletchley. Except for the time when the group was at Beaumanor, all log sheets reached them by despatch rider. The messages were sent to Hut 6, also by despatch rider, for a good part of the war.

Unfortunately the term 'Traffic Analysis' or TA, when applied to wartime radio nets carrying Enigma traffic, means different things to different people. To some it means obtaining information from a study of the logs. To others it involves enciphered Enigma messages as well as the chit-chat in the logs. When I used the term in my book I meant the analysis of enciphered Enigma messages and their preambles. This, from the outset, was done in Hut 6. The log-reading was done by the M18 group, who ultimately joined forces with Hut 6.

Without going into too much detail I want to show that our method of handling message analysis, well established in the first year and virtually unchanged throughout the war, mattered a great deal. It was based on the 'Traffic Register', which should perhaps have been called the 'Message Register'. It contained the preamble of each message and the first six letters of enciphered text. This was all that we needed in Hut 6 until we decided how we were going to attempt to break a daily key. The register was sent, page by page, by teleprinter, so there was very little delay between the interception of a message and the time at which its preamble reached Hut 6.

Until May 1940 the register revealed female indicators. Then it enabled us to work immediately on Herivel tips and Cillis. Later on it enabled us to call for important messages to be sent to Hut 6 by teleprinter rather than by despatch rider.

In Hut 6 three copies of the register went to three destinations, to the Registration room, where the messages were charted, to the cryptological wizards, who used them to plan their attempts at breaks, and to Colman's team of intercept co-ordinators, who used them in their constant telephone contacts with duty officers at the intercept stations, who had their own copies of the register pages that they had transmitted. It proved to be a very speedy and efficient system of information exchange between the specialised teams whose contributions were essential to our success. From Jean's research it now seems that leading people in Hut 3 did not realise how this Traffic Register system reduced the delays involved both in breaking and in giving them the most important decodes. It also seems that Oeser and other leaders in Hut 3 contributed little. But there was probably not much that they could do. When the heyday of Ultra had arrived, Milner-Barry's team of wizards, Colman's team of co-ordinators, the large log-reading effort, and the experienced people at the intercept stations could do a good job on their own. It was extremely important that this group of teams were allowed to collaborate without uninformed outside interference.

Indeed the British success in developing and using Hut 6 Ultra was largely due to the early establishment of excellent communication, collaboration and co-operation between many specialised activities. In Chapter 3 of *The Ultra Secret*, Winterbotham recalls how the intelligence part of the overall plan was born. Menzies showed him the 'first results' from Bletchley – four decodes of German air force Enigma messages – and asked him to take them to the Director of Air Intelligence at the Air Ministry. On the following morning Winterbotham presented Menzies with a plan for handling the output of Hut 6. Anticipating problems that would arise later, he proposed that an intelligence organisation be set up at Bletchley to work closely with Hut 6, and also that Special Liaison Units (SLUs) be established to protect the security of Ultra in the field. Menzies said, 'All right, you can go ahead if you can get the approval of the Directors of Intelligence'. The Director of Air Intelligence gave his approval immediately. Then, says Winterbotham, 'As luck would have it,

THE BIRTH OF ULTRA

the next signals to be caught and unbuttoned were from the German Army'.

So he approached the Director of Military Intelligence at the War Office and won his immediate approval. Thus, within a few days, it became possible to establish an inter service intelligence activity at Bletchley and to start building up an organisation of SLUs. That this was achieved so early proved to be of immense importance. However, writing from memory, after more than 30 years, Winterbotham got his dates wrong. He made it seem that all this happened in early April 1940. This error was repeated by Lewin,[52] who also gave the erroneous impression that Hut 6 was not put on a 24-hour footing until just before Hitler's invasion of Denmark and Norway. Hinsley repeats both these errors in his official history. Fortunately a glimpse of the true story is provided by a list of the broken Enigma keys that were exchanged between Bruno and Bletchley during the period of co-operation. It now seems that Hut 6 Ultra was born in mid-January 1940, not in early April.

VIII

LANGER'S LIST OF 126 BROKEN ENIGMA KEYS

Colonel Langer wrote a 48-page report – probably in Algeria in autumn 1940 – on the activities of his Cipher Bureau. This report contains a listing of broken Enigma keys, which is shown in a modified form in Tables 1 and 2. Table 1 starts with the last daily key broken in Poland before the war – a key for 6 July 1939, broken on 26 August, 1939. The other entries in Table 1 are daily keys of 1939 broken at Bruno or Bletchley in 1940.

Table 2 is concerned with daily keys of 1940. In this table it has been convenient to show the delay in days between the date of a daily key and its entry in Langer's list of broken keys. Polish breaks would have been recorded at once, but Bletchley breaks could not be entered until they had been communicated to Bruno, which evidently took many days in the early months of collaboration.

Unfortunately Langer's list does not indicate which of the German crypto nets (Red, Green or Blue) was involved in each break. Nor does it say which of the breaks were achieved at Bruno. But we have clues, and it is intriguing to speculate on what may have happened.

In his rebuttal of much of the content of Hinsley's Appendix 1 to Volume 1,[53] Rejewski agrees that 83 per cent of the keys in Langer's list were broken at Bletchley. This means a score of 105 for Bletchley and 21 for Bruno. He also points out that at Bruno everything had to be done by Zygalski, Rozycki and himself, whereas Bletchley already had far more people at work. Indeed the Polish achievement of 21 breaks is quite remarkable, remembering that this same team of three would be deciphering messages on daily keys broken at Bletchley.

It seems clear that the first break at Bruno was the daily key for 28 October 1939, broken on 17 January 1940, immediately after the arrival of perforated sheets from Bletchley. This was the Green key used by the administrative centres of the German army. It also seems clear, though surprising to me, that the Green key for 25 October 1939 was broken at Bletchley at about the same time.[54] Apart from this one key I suggest that the remaining nine daily keys of Table 1 were Polish breaks.

TABLE 1
DAILY KEYS OF 1939
(shown on Langer's List of Breaks)

Date of Daily Key (in 1939)	Date of Break
July 6	August 26 1939
August 2	January ? 1940
September 3	January 28
September 10	March 17
September 13	March 17
September 19	February 28
September 29	February 23
September 30	February 13
October 25	January 27
October 28	January 17

In the period covered by Table 2, there are 16 cases in which two different daily keys for the same day were broken. I suggest that the Poles broke the first of the keys shown in the table for the following seven days: 6, 16, 18, 26 January, 24, 27 February and 20 March; also that they broke the second keys on five days: 18 January, 21 February and 2, 21, 27 March. This accounts for the Bruno score of 21 breaks. Those shown on Table 2 are italicised. Much of this is pure conjecture, but it may well be pretty accurate.

It appears that, after the sheets were received on 17 January 1940, the Polish three-man team worked backwards, leaving work on current keys to Bletchley. I suspect that they concentrated on Green traffic, while we concentrated on Red. As I discovered in my studies of September and October 1939, the French intercept stations were far better placed for the interception of Green traffic than was our station at Chatham under Commander Ellingworth.[55] Furthermore, I found that the call signs were repeated monthly, so the French traffic analysts, as a result of observation over a long period, would have been able to provide a complete forecast of call signs for each day. This would have been a great help to

TABLE 2

DELAYS IN DAYS BETWEEN THE DATE OF A DAILY KEY OF 1940 AND ITS ENTRY ON LANGER'S LIST OF BROKEN KEYS

Date of Daily Key	Delays Jan. A	Delays Jan. B	Delays Feb. A	Delays Feb. B	Delays March A	Delays March B	Delays April A	Delays April B	Delays May A	Delays May B	Delays June A	Delays June B
1					14				1		0	
2					6	24			0			
3							1		1			
4					7	14			2		0	
5									7		0	
6	19				5				1		0	
7					4				2		0	
8			15		4		1		1		0	
9					2		3	6	1			
10							4	4	1			
11							1		1		0	
12			15		4	5	4		1		0	
13			14		4	8			1		0	
14			9				2		1		1	
15							1				6	
16	43		10		2		1				5	
17	11						1					
18	34	41					2					
19							1	5				
20			6		17		1		1			
21			7	23	2	19	1	1	0			
22	12		4		8	11	1	1	1			
23			8		3		1	2	1			
24	15		23				1		1			
25					8		1	1	0			
26	28						1		1			
27			31		2	13	0		0			
28							2		1			
29	10		4				1		0			
30	14		X		9		1		1			
31	5		X				X		0			

Columns A and B allow for cases in which two different daily keys for the same day were broken.

intercept operators because, as Ellingworth explained to me, the German radio net carrying Green traffic used an unusual method of operation which made it difficult to intercept.[56] Anyway, using available Green intercepts, the Poles attacked the Green key for 6 January 1940, which they broke on 19 January, only two days after the arrival of the perforated sheets. Next, on 28 January, having no doubt spent a lot of time decoding messages on the two broken keys, they broke the Green key for 3 September 1939. In February and March of 1940 they went back to Green traffic of 30, 29, 19, 13, and 10 September 1939. This is shown in Table 1.

They also managed to attack current traffic of several days in January, February and March of 1940, as shown in Table 2: a truly remarkable achievement by Rejewski, Zygalski and Rozcyki.

Because I have no recollection whatever of an early break of Green in Hut 6, I think that the Bletchley break of the Green key for 25 October 1939 must have been made in the Cottage around 17 January when a complete set of perforated sheets had become available. The Hut 6 activities were based on intercepts received from Chatham, and I am pretty certain that these would not have permitted a break of Green at that time. On the other hand French intercepts may well have been made available to Dilly's team in the Cottage.[57]

Let us suppose that, after completion of the Jeffreys sheets, the first two Bletchley breaks, both made in the Cottage, were the Red key of 17 January 1940,[58] and the Green key of 25 October 1939. This would tie in with Winterbotham's account of the Enigma decodes that Menzies showed him.

As yet, I have not been able to determine just when Jeffreys, with his team and their sheets, moved from the Cottage to Hut 6. It was certainly before 29 January 1940, when John Herivel arrived at Bletchley and found Hut 6 operational on a 24-hour footing. He remembers that early in February, when he had got the hang of the machine, he was concerned by our lack of success (the table shows no breaks between 31 December and 8 February) and found himself continually thinking about what could be done about it. Then, one evening in his digs, when he was imagining what it would be like to be a German operator preparing to send off his first message of the day, the idea of his 'tip' flashed into his mind. His recollection, however, is that the tip did not become significant until the German Blitzkrieg of 10 May 1940, when suddenly a number of German operators simultaneously showed the appropriate form of laziness.

Looking at Table 2, it seems possible that the move to Hut 6 occurred between 17 and 22 January, and that the broken keys of 22, 24, 29, 30 and 31 January were Red. But I am still puzzled by my memory that the first Hut 6 break was into the Blue crypto net used for training.[59] Perhaps the key for 22 January was of Blue and the double breaks of March were of Red and Blue.[60] I feel sure that the 24-hour operation of the supporting activities in Hut 6 had started before Jeffreys arrived, in fact in early January 1940, or in late December 1939.[61] This was one of the things that really mattered.

We now come to the spectacular changes in Langer's listing that occurred in April, May and June of 1940. Going by the delays in Langer's recordings of Bletchley breaks, it seems that direct teletype communications between Bletchley and Bruno were not established until late March or early April. More important is the fact that regular breaking of Red

THE BIRTH OF ULTRA

traffic began on 8 April, when the Phoney War ended with preparations for the invasion of Denmark and Norway on the following day.[62]

The gap in breaking between 14 and 20 May was, of course, caused by the German change of procedure, which made our perforated sheets useless.[63] Note that the date on which the change became effective was 15 May, which fits in with my memory, not the commonly accepted 10 May, the day on which Hitler's invasion was launched. Indeed, as was shown in section V.1 above, the Germans seem to have developed a habit of making major changes on the fifteenth day of a month.

The resumption of Hut 6 breaking on 20 May, after a lapse of only five days, was not due, as Hinsley claims on page 494 of his Volume 1, to the arrival of the first bombes. It was due to German operators who, working no doubt under unprecedented pressure, suddenly made the Herivel tip effective and provided enough Cillis to exploit it. Note the increasing number of zeros in Langer's list. This was due to the fact that the Herivel tip depended on the first messages sent by lazy operators after a midnight key change. With the old method we had to wait until enough female indicators had appeared before we could start stacking perforated sheets. Now, if German operators provided enough Cillis as well as a good Herivel tip, the break of a daily Red key could sometimes be achieved in Hut 6 by the midnight to 8 a.m. watch. Again, as with the old method, the Traffic Register from Chatham provided our Machine Room with all the necessary information.

It may seem barely credible, but comparable success, using the Herivel–Cillis method, was maintained until the actual arrival of the bombes. On page 184 of his Volume 1, Hinsley contradicts his other statement, saying that the first bombe was delivered in August 1940, but I suspect that it may have been even later. My guess would be that the bombes did not begin to be effective until September 1940. We were indeed lucky.

REFERENCES

References are given in chronological order of publication. Not all are mentioned in the article.

1. David Kahn, *The Codebreakers: The Story of Secret Writing* (London: Weidenfeld & Nicolson, 1967).
2. J.C. Masterson, *The Double-Cross System in the War of 1939–45* (New Haven: Yale University Press, 1972).
3. David Kahn, *The Codebreakers* (abridged) (London: Sphere, 1973).
4. Gustave Bertrand, *Enigma, The Greatest Riddle of World War II* (Paris: Plon, 1973).
5. F.W. Winterbotham, *The Ultra Secret* (London: Weidenfeld & Nicolson, 1974).
6. Anthony Cave Brown, *Bodyguard of Lies* (London: W.H. Allen, 1975).
7. William Stevenson, *A Man Called Intrepid: The Secret War* (London: Macmillan, 1976).

8. Penelope Fitzgerald, *The Knox Brothers* (London: Macmillan, 1977).
9. Ronald Lewin, *Ultra Goes to War: The Secret Story* (London: Hutchinson, 1978).
10. David Kahn, *Hitler's Spies: German Military Intelligence in World War II* (London: Hodder & Stoughton, 1978).
11. Brian Johnson, *The Secret War* (London: BBC Publications, 1978).
12. R.V. Jones, *Most Secret War* (London: Hamish Hamilton, 1978).
13. Wladyslaw Kozaczuk, *W Kregu Enigmy* (Warsaw: Ksiazka i Wiedza, 1979).
14. F.H. Hinsley, *British Intelligence in the Second World War* (London: HMSO, Volume 1, 1979; Volume 2, 1981).
15. 'The Polish, French and British Contributions to the Breaking of the Enigma' (Appendix 1 to Vol. 1 of ref. 14 above, 1979).
16. Ralph Bennett, *Ultra in the West* (New York: Scribner, 1979).
17. Jozef Garlinski, *The Enigma War* (published as *Intercept*, London: Dent & Sons, 1979); (New York: Scribner, 1980).
18. Peter Calvocoressi, *Top Secret Ultra* (London: Cassell, 1980).
19. Jean Stengers, 'La Guerre des Messages Codés (1930–1945)', in *L'Histoire*, February 1981.
20. Marian Rejewski, 'How Polish Mathematicians Deciphered the Enigma' (published posthumously in Polish in Poland, 1980), translation published in *Annals of the History of Computing*, July 1981. (Another translation published as Appendix D in ref. 30, 1984.)
21. Marian Rejewski, 'Mathematical Solution of the Enigma Cipher' (published posthumously in Polish in ref. 13, 1979), translation published in *Cryptologia*, January 1982, and copied as Appendix E in ref. 30, 1984.
22. Christopher Kasparek and Richard A. Woytak, 'In Memoriam Marian Rejewski', *Cryptologia*, January 1982. (Part of it appears as Appendix A in ref. 30, 1984.)
23. Wladyslaw Kozaczuk, 'Enigma Solved' (excerpts from ref. 30) in *Cryptologia*, January 1982.
24. Richard A. Woytak, 'A Conversation with Marian Rejewski' in *Cryptologia*, January 1982 (recorded on tape in Polish, 24 July 1978, and reproduced as Appendix B in ref. 30, 1984).
25. Marian Rejewski, 'Remarks on Appendix 1 to *British Intelligence in the Second World War* by F.H. Hinsley' (letter to Woytak) in *Cryptologia*, January 1982.
26. Gordon Welchman, *The Hut Six Story: Breaking the Enigma Codes* (London: Allen Lane; New York: McGraw Hill, 1982).
27. Ronald Lewin, *American Magic* (New York: Farrar, Straus & Giraux, 1982).
28. Andrew Hodges, *Alan Turing – The Enigma* (London: Burnett Books, 1983).
29. Jean Stengers, 'Enigma, the French, the Poles and the British, 1931–1940' in C. Andrew and D. Dilks (eds.), *The Missing Dimension* (London: Macmillan, 1984).
30. Wladyslaw Kozaczuk, *Enigma – How the German Machine Cipher was Broken and How it was Read by the Allies in World War Two, with Appendices A to F* (edited and translated by Christopher Kasparek, London: Arms and Armour Press, 1984).

NOTES

1. See ref. 4.
2. See ref. 5.
3. See ref. 26.
4. See ref. 19.
5. See ref. 17. It was called *Intercept* in the UK, where it was published in 1979.
6. See ref. 21.
7. See ref. 20.
8. See ref. 29.
9. See ref. 30.
10. See ref. 13.
11. See ref. 15.

THE BIRTH OF ULTRA

12. See ref. 28.
13. See Chapter 5, *The Hut Six Story*.
14. *The Hut Six Story*, pp. 170–76.
15. When I was writing *The Hut Six Story* I knew nothing of the work in the Cottage on Cillis. I called them sillies, and my account of how they worked is quite wrong. This was pointed out to me by Dennis Babbage, who was an expert. The correct account is far more fascinating. After reading my book, Lisicki told me of a somewhat similar method known to the Poles as 'the Knox Method'.
16. See ref. 9.
17. See ref. 27.
18. Kozaczuk, *Enigma*, p. 235.
19. *The Hut Six Story*, p. 16.
20. Ibid., p. 13.
21. In my discussion of the Bletchley Park environment I mentioned that the expression 'cock and bull story' is said to have originated in Stony Stratford, where there are two famous pubs, the Cock and the Bull. *The Hut Six Story*, p. 187.
22. In Kozaczuk, *Enigma*, pp. 249 and 276 respectively.
23. Ibid., p. 249.
24. These drums are described in *The Hut Six Story*, pp. 307 and 308. Similar drums appear in the picture of the American version of the bombe in Lewin, *The American Magic*, facing p. 142.
25. See *The Hut Six Story*, pp. 38ff.
26. Their method of operation is discussed in *The Hut Six Story*, pp. 153–6.
27. Some writers have used the word 'setting' to mean the daily key.
28. *The Hut Six Story*, p. 169.
29. Kozaczuk, *Enigma*, p. 265.
30. Ibid., p. 246.
31. *The Hut Six Story*, p. 46.
32. Ibid., p. 50.
33. See Kozaczuk, *Enigma*, p. 258.
34. Ibid., pp. 284 and 285.
35. Ibid., p. 264.
36. Ibid., p. 266.
37. The construction of the bomba is indicated by Rejewski in Figure E–8, Kozaczuk, *Enigma*, p. 289.
38. His train of thought is indicated in Kozaczuk, *Enigma*, p. 287.
39. The principle is more fully explained in *The Hut Six Story*, Chapter 4. A Zygalski sheet is illustrated in Figure E–7 in Kozaczuk, *Enigma*, p. 288.
40. They had been issued in 1936 with the idea that they would be brought into use when war became imminent. Kozaczuk, *Enigma*, p. 64.
41. Calvocoressi (see ref. 18) was incorrect in saying that, at this time, no one in the world could read messages enciphered on the five-wheel Enigma.
42. Kozaczuk, *Enigma*, p. 236.
43. Ibid., p. 257.
44. *The Hut Six Story*, p. 307.
45. Kozaczuk, *Enigma*, p. 97.
46. *The Hut Six Story*, p. 100.
47. Kozaczuk, *Enigma*, p. 60.
48. *The Hut Six Story*, p. 131.
49. This statement was not used in the BBC programme for the anniversary of D-Day. This was perhaps just as well, because Jean had been given a lot of misinformation.
50. See ref. 18.
51. See *The Hut Six Story*, Chapter 9. The chit-chat used the international Q-Codes, still widely used today (p. 154).
52. See Lewin, *Ultra Goes To War*, p. 60.
53. See *Cryptologia*, Vol. VI, No. 1 (January 1982), pp. 74–83.
54. The date of this Bletchley break is stated to be 18 January 1940, on p. 662 of Hinsley's

Volume 2. However, his earlier account in Vol. 1, p. 493, is, I believe, inaccurate.
55. *The Hut Six Story*, p. 54.
56. The monthly repeat of call signs was discontinued soon after I discovered it.
57. I was given large bundles of these intercepts in September 1939. See *The Hut Six Story*, p. 54.
58. I think that Hinsley was misinformed in stating that the Red key for 6 January 1940 was broken at Bletchley on the same day.
59. *The Hut Six Story*, p. 88.
60. Hinsley, vol. 2, p. 659, gives 29 January as the date on which Blue was first broken, but he gives 6 January for Red which seem wrong.
61. *The Hut Six Story*, p. 89.
62. The second breaks into keys for 9, 10, 19, 21, 22, 23 and 25 may have been into the Yellow key, which, according to Hinsley (Vol. 2, p. 662) was first broken on 10 April. I have no recollection of the introduction by the German army of a second crypto net for operations in Norway. The key that we broke regularly from 8 April on was certainly the Red key, used in battle for army–air co-ordination. To me the Yellow crypto net is still a puzzle.
63. *The Hut Six Story*, p. 97.

Ultra's Poor Relations

CHRISTOPHER MORRIS

'Operation Cinderella'. The two words appeared briefly on the door of a room at Bletchley Park during the Second World War. It was the room occupied by one particular party, of which I happened to be a member. The words were at once symptomatic and prophetic. They were symptomatic of the rather low state of morale from which the party suffered on occasion. They were prophetic of the somewhat meagre place which their work now holds in the published annals of Bletchley Park's achievements.

The work in question was work on German naval hand ciphers. But it can, very probably, be regarded as a fair sample of work on enemy hand ciphers in general. In any case, it is the only work of which I can write with first-hand knowledge, although inevitably what I write is bound to have an autobiographical flavour, and bound also to be largely a mere worm's-eye view. It is, however, based on a lengthy memorandum which I wrote at the bidding of my head of section before I left Bletchley in the late summer of 1945; and that memorandum was based on all the relevant documents then available to me, as well as on the spoken or written evidence of numerous colleagues.

Our eyes are still so dazzled by the miracle of Ultra, by the prodigies of mathematical thinking which went into the deciphering of the various German Enigma machines, that very naturally the historians have not noticed and the public have not known that the Germans also made use of rather numerous hand ciphers of varying degrees of complexity. This tunnel vision applies perhaps most of all to naval operations; for the German navy's Enigma machine was the hardest nut to crack, the last to be broken, and possibly the most important because of its bearing on the U-boat war. Naval Ultra therefore held and still holds a peculiarly dazzling character – so much so that very few people are aware that in the course of the war the German navy used no less than 27 different hand ciphers, six of them high-grade. The traffic in three of the high-grade ciphers was read, quite often currently, for the greater part of their life-spans; and so was the traffic in the majority of the lesser ciphers.

Some at least of the deciphered signals have claims to value or importance – an importance of three different kinds. The signals could be a major source of 'cribs' into *Schluessel* M, the Enigma machine, since the same facts or orders were often transmitted in more than one cipher. The signals could contain quite valuable information, occasionally even information of operational importance. They had, too, a certain historical importance because, such was the pessimism of the authorities at the outset, unless there had been some early breaks into certain hand ciphers, serious work on German naval ciphers as a whole might never have begun. Something needs to be said under each of these headings.

SIGNALS AS A SOURCE OF 'CRIBS'

Long after the structure of the Enigma machine became known (and even after a machine was captured) the setting for each successive day had to be discovered. This was not always achieved by pure mathematical analysis nor yet solely by the 'Bombe', the rudimentary computer invented for the purpose. It helped greatly to know the likely content and if possible the exact initial wording of a particular signal. There is indeed no such thing as absolutely 'pure' cryptanalysis. To know that a signal is in German, or that in German 'e' is the commonest letter, or that the signal is on a naval wireless frequency, or that it is likely to be about the weather is, in each case, to have a partial or potential 'crib'. The cryptographer, like all discoverers, must proceed from the known to the unknown.

The German navy was for a long time quite liberal in providing 'cribs'. 'Cribs' were in fact almost inevitable unless all naval vessels, from battleships to tugs, had been confined to the use of one single cipher. But auxiliaries and small craft did not carry *Schluessel* M, whereas U-boats normally used nothing else. Consequently a storm-warning or a notice that some swept channel had been mined had to be transmitted both in Enigma and in something else – usually in *Werftschluessel* (literally Dockyard Key) hereinafter to be called W/S. For many months the German cipher clerks took too little care to vary the wording, word-order or spelling in such signals. Had they but known it, ringing the changes between '*fuenf*' and '*funf*' or between '*nul*' and '*null*' would have added considerably to our problems.

As both a typical and principal provider of 'cribs' W/S deserves a brief discursus. Traffic in it was first detected in April 1940, and the first decipherment from it some months later was produced by fitting on a 'crib' provided in a captured document. After that the signals were deciphered by various cryptographic techniques unassisted by the capture of any keys or tables. 'Cryptographic' was the word used at the time for what is now usually called 'cryptanalytic'. W/S traffic was read at first retrospectively but by March 1941 as a rule currently, until by February 1945 the traffic had become so negligible both in volume and in content as to be deemed not worth deciphering. The continuous reading of it constitutes easily the long-distance record among German naval hand ciphers. About 33,000 signals in W/S were read, over 30,000 of them currently, covering a period of 47 months, averaging 23 signals a day.

The traffic consisted of five-letter groups, for which the clear text had been written out in vertical columns, each five letters wide, and enciphered by substituting for each vertical pair of letters another bigram taken from a substitution table, using a separate table for each of the five columns.

T H E P L	A L C O L
A I N T E	U M N S F
X T O F T	I V E L E
H E S I G	T T E R S
N A L I S	W I D E L
W R I T T	I K E T H
E N I N V	I S X Y Z
E R T I C	P Q R S T

There were 20 tables at first and later 30, a new *Heft* or set of tables being provided at first every two months and later every month. During the cipher's lifetime the cryptographers of German Naval Section had to reconstruct the 20 or 30 new tables 38 times.

The substituted bigrams were reciprocal, that is, if AB became XY in one table, then XY in that table would become AB. Moreover, neither letter of any bigram reappeared in its substitute; e.g. AB could not become AX or XB, nor yet XA or BX. All of these phenomena, had the Germans but known it, made the cryptographer's task a fraction easier. The cryptographers relied on a reasonable 'depth', that is, number and length of signals, on informed or intelligent guesses at the content of certain signals, recognised from external characteristics as likely to be of a routine nature. 'Cribs' of course were almost essential when a new *Heft* came into use. It was also possible to exploit repetitions in the same column of certain common bigrams such as EE, EN, NE, and so on. EE occurs twice in the English sample given above, as it does in the word MESSA or the word BLETC. EE is at least equally common in German,
GE   HLEY
e.g. in FREIG or BEDEU.
     EGEBE   TEN
     N

The beginning of this poem by Goethe may be taken as an illustration of vertical repeats – admittedly perhaps an extreme case.

I	C	H	D	E
N	K	E	D	E
I	N	W	E	N
N	M	I	R	D
E	R	S	O	N·
N	E	S	C	H
I	M	M	E	R
V	O	M	M	E
E	R	E	S	T
R	A	H	L	T
I	C	H	D	E
N	K	E	D	E
I	N	W	E	N
N	S	I	C	H
D	E	S	M	O
N	D	E	S	F
L	I	M	M	E
R	I	N	Q	U
E	L	L	E	N
M	A	L	T	

It will be noted that in column 1 IN occurs four times, that in column 3 HE and WI occur twice each and that in column 5 EE occurs twice.

Once the content of a signal was known or guessed, other vertical bigram repeats could be recognised, even of relatively uncommon letters, e.g. the FS in

     FEUER
     SCHIF
     FFLEN
     SBURG

To go into further detail might lead me to poach on 'classified' preserves.

Since W/S was the cipher used by all minor naval vessels in German home waters and, after the fall of Norway and of France, in Norwegian and Biscayan waters (though not in the Channel, no doubt through fear of capture), it soon became apparent that *Schluessel* M and W/S could and did provide 'cribs' into one another when the same information or instructions were transmitted in both ciphers. Indeed the 'cross-ruffing' between the two was for some time the prize exhibit which Naval Section could display to distinguished visitors, such as Winston Churchill in September 1941.

The heyday of W/S as a main source of 'cribs' lasted throughout 1942 and into 1943; and during this period whenever it was proving difficult to break into a new set of W/S tables or into a new complication of the Enigma machine, Operation 'Garden' would be set in motion. This meant mine-laying in the known German swept channels and would invariably provoke *Sperrnachrichten* announcing that such and such a *weg* was '*gesperrt*' between two specified and numbered points. These furnished ideal 'cribs'; and 'Gardening' would sometimes be laid on if the reading of home waters Enigma was wanted in a hurry, as it would be if an Arctic convoy was about to sail.

INFORMATION OF OPERATIONAL IMPORTANCE

Other hand ciphers from time to time supplied 'cribs' into one another or into something higher grade but W/S was unrivalled in this field. Nor was its content wholly uninteresting. Any major ship addressing an auxiliary had to do so in W/S. Consequently almost every German warship from the *Tirpitz* down to destroyers used it on occasion and thereby told us her whereabouts; once, when we had lost track of the *Scheer* for some weeks she made a W/S signal reporting on the weather near Danzig. Above all, it was often possible to learn from W/S that a new U-boat had been commissioned and was exercising in the Baltic. The same cipher could also tell us of the routing of coastal convoys, of damage suffered by German shipping, of the movements of hospital ships and transports serving the German army on the Eastern front, and not least the volume of east or westbound traffic in the Baltic. More than half the W/S signals deciphered were thought worth teleprinting to the Admiralty.

The longest serving members of the W/S party were John Barns (later to become a notable papyrologist), Paul Smither (a very promising young Egyptologist who, tragically, had to leave Bletchley early in 1943 to die of leukaemia – but not before he had invented a most ingenious cryptographic device known as the 'key-finder' which greatly expedited the discovery of the five tables used in each signal), Ruth Briggs, now Mrs Oliver Churchill, (an excellent young German scholar from Newnham who became probably the party's most reliable all-round performer), Philip Hunt (a young PPE graduate who went later into the Board of Trade), Roland Oliver (still an undergraduate but later to be a professor of African history), and myself. It should be added that whenever more labourers were needed in the vineyard, that is, when a new set of Hefts had to be broken, Dr C.T. Carr, later to be Professor of German at St Andrews, would lend his aid, leaving his work on other hand ciphers.

Another high-grade naval hand cipher that was read for a considerable time, from September 1939 to May 1941 (though not currently till April 1940), was *Schluessel* H, known to Naval Section as 'Merchant Navy'. It was used by Merchant Navy ships controlled by the German Admiralty. The cipher in its earlier form consisted of bigram substitution, horizontal or vertical, on a text composed of groups drawn from the International Code of Signals (the Merchant Navy Code Book). The cipher was broken almost single-handed by Professor W. H. Bruford, largely by analysis, though assisted for a time by the capture of one set of bigram tables. Most signals contained lacunae requiring some ingenuity to complete. After mid-1941 the systems used became so complex as to be deemed unbreakable, at any rate with the labour then available. Since *Schluessel* H provided the earliest naval signals in a high-grade cipher that were read at Bletchley it caused rather more stir than its normal content really warranted. Indeed in April 1940 the actual workings of two tyro cryptographers (Paul Smither and myself) were sent up to the Admiralty to show what Bletchley's Naval Section could now do. The signal only gave Oxeloesund, Sweden, as the destination of a German merchant ship of moderate tonnage.

The excitement thus engendered can be understood only if we recall the pessimism long maintained in high quarters about the possibility of any deciphering of German naval signals. During the Munich crisis it was noticed that German naval signal-traffic had been reduced to a very bare minimum. From this Admiral Sinclair, then head of SIS, deduced that in the event of war the Germany navy would maintain total wireless silence 'and that therefore this organisation of ours is useless for the purpose for which it was intended'. In view of this it may not be wholly surprising that in September 1939 the German Naval Section at GC & CS consisted of precisely two persons, neither of them a cryptographer. For months the Section, even when enlarged to ten or twelve persons, fumbled in gross darkness. The first deciphered signal that ever came its way and threw any light on the German navy was a police message concerning the punishment of a drunken cook in a *Vorpostenboot*. Since it was not previously realised that ships of that designation existed, the Section realised that it still had much to learn.

COUNTERING OFFICIAL PESSIMISM

But the first feather the Section could put in its own cap was plucked from a strange bird, not really a sea-bird and one whose capture did not involve the highest form of cryptanalysis. This was the virtually self-evident *Flugmeldesignal* reporting enemy aircraft, and enabling us to work out the German 'grid'. Naval officers were said to be impressed by the ability of German Naval Section to say that FLG meant *Flugzeug* (aeroplane) or that SOT meant *Sudost* (southeast).

Even after these modest triumphs pessimism continued to prevail. As late as the summer of 1940 I myself heard Commander Denniston, head of GC & CS, saying to the head of Naval Section, 'You know, the Germans don't mean you to read their stuff, and I don't suppose you ever will.' The Section was in fact caught in a vicious circle. It could not get adequate staff without first achieving successes, and it could achieve little success without adequate staff. At first, too, even when potential cryptographers were recruited, for many months they were seconded for more than half their time to other duties such as nocturnal watch-keeping, logging incoming intercepts, learning to interpret wireless traffic from its external characteristics, or commuting to the Admiralty to explain and sell such wares as Bletchley could provide.

Even when some successes had been achieved, the cryptographers laboured under certain disadvantages. An experience of my own will furnish an example. In mid-April 1940 I deciphered a 'Merchant Navy' signal, for which I claim no credit; I was simply doing what Professor Bruford told me and performing an almost mechanical operation. The signal ordered all ships bound for Bergen to report their positions at stated intervals to the German War Office. I was told that ships do not report to War Offices, so would I please correct the error. I had my workings checked and the text remained the same. The ships were of course troop-ships, and the signal could have given us advance notice of the invasion of Norway. But I have found no evidence that the signal was ever sent to the Admiralty, and it is certainly unmentioned in the history books. The reason is that hand cipher was on the whole distrusted and graded for reliability well below Enigma – on the grounds that it is human to err whereas the machine cannot lie. Actually, for technical reasons, if a letter has been incorrectly transmitted, received or copied, it is more easily checked if it is in a bigram substitution cipher than it would be in Enigma. This undervaluing of hand ciphers had quite far-reaching repercussions. As will be shown, it distinctly limited their potential utility and it seriously lowered the cryptographers' morale. But I must first complete my survey of Naval Section's relatively successful work on the enemy's hand ciphers.

One high grade cipher of considerable value, both for intelligence purposes and for the supply of 'cribs', was the *Reservehandverfahren* (RHV) used by the Germans if and when the Enigma machine broke down, and by some ships instead of the machine. RHV involved transposing the clear text through a 'cage' and then applying vertical bigram substitution to the transposed text on four different substitution tables. It was first read, through a captured document, in June 1941 and later rebroken by cryptographic methods. Traffic in it was read, more or less currently, for some 40 months, the volume amounting to about 1400 signals averaging 12 per day; although once, for two days in July 1943, all German North Sea signals (perhaps through fear that *Schluessel* M might be compromised) were transmitted in RHV. U-boats carried their own separate RHV transposition 'cages', in case their machines proved faulty or were thought unsafe. This system was known to the Germans as

'Offizier'. Only six of such signals were diagnosed at Bletchley with any certainty and all were deciphered (three of them by James Hogarth), two of these giving the current recognition signal schedule.

Prominent among those who worked on RHV were J.H. Plumb (later Professor Sir John Plumb the historian), A.S.C. Ross (later to be associated with 'U' and 'non-U' speech), Dr C.T. Carr already mentioned, Bentley Bridgewater (later Secretary to the British Museum) and James Hogarth (later to be a high official in the Scottish Office). Hogarth arrived at Bletchley as a Private. He soon proved too indispensable to be allowed to go to an OCTU to become an officer. But, meriting rapid promotion, he ended the war as a Regimental Sergeant Major, although few men have had a less military bearing or physique.

In the Mediterranean the Germans had a separate form of RHV known as *Schluessel Henno*, enciphered on the same system but with different transposition cages and bigram tables. It first appeared in May 1943 and work on it was at first unsuccessful and was temporarily abandoned. But in April 1944 all the Henno documents were captured in a raid on Mykonos. The Germans must have realised that the cipher was compromised, and they began immediately and rapidly to change transposition 'cages', bigram tables etc. one by one. Had they changed all at once they might well have prevented, or at least seriously delayed, any deciphering. As it was, Naval Section was just able to keep pace with them, but shortage of manpower meant that not all current traffic and very little 'back stuff' could be dealt with. The volume of Henno signals amounted to over 1,000 per month. At one time as many as 30 people were at work on the cipher. It was the Section's most impressive mass attack. Nevertheless the intelligence value of Henno, with a few exceptions, proved rather disappointing; and by the end of August 1944, not without a good deal of controversy, work on Henno was abandoned.

INVISIBLE EXPORTS

No account of the work undertaken by the cryptographers of Naval Section would be complete without some reference to their by-products or invisible exports. These fall into two classes: (1) ciphers which were deemed more suitable for handling elsewhere; (2) ciphers which did not strictly belong to German Naval Section but which the Section's cryptographers worked on in their spare time or in slack periods.

An example of the first class was the *Funkverkehrsheft*, a three-letter book, frequently randomised or 're-hatted', used by harbour defence flotillas on all German-occupied coasts (especially the Channel Islands). The cipher was partially read from its beginning in mid-1941, partly from 'cribs' and eventually from a captured code-book. The signals included reports of German aircraft crossing the French or Dutch coasts en route for the UK. For this reason relevant decodes were sent to Bletchley's Air Section and/or to coastal stations rather than to the Admiralty, thus constituting an invisible export.

A related cipher *Funkverkehrsheft Kueste* (known as 'K code' at Bletchley), also a three-letter book 're-hatted', was used from December 1942 by coastal batteries and radar stations in the Channel and Mediterranean. As it was an inter-service code there was some difficulty in getting any one British service to acknowledge responsibility and pay for the infant's upbringing, but the foundling ended up on Naval Section's doorstep. The decodes were sent to Alexandria and, after D-Day, to 21st Army Group in Normandy. There is a legend, still unconfirmed, that in the small hours of D-Day the solitary K-code signal from a shore station in the battle area said 'Cancel state of readiness'.

A similar code (three-letter book), simpler because neither frequently nor radically changed, was the *Seenotfunksignaltafel* (SN), used and read for three years from July 1940. It was designed merely to delay deciphering and to be very quickly read by its German recipients. Its purpose was to provide a rescue service for aircraft coming to grief in the Channel. In practice if the aircraft 'ditched' in our half of the Channel, the British 'crash-boat' often arrived on the scene before the enemy's. To facilitate rapid exploitation the handling of this code was given to Dover Command and dealt with on the spot. Much of the work on all of these ciphers was done by Dr Carr, assisted by Jean Watt (née Donaldson) and later by Sheila Mackenzie.

Other kinds of invisible export arose from quite different causes. The work of the cryptographer can fluctuate. At times the volume of readable traffic necessitates a call for all hands to the pump. But at other periods the traffic may become temporarily unreadable or the stream of traffic, though readable, may dwindle to a trickle. This can easily occur during a night shift. A conscientious cryptographer with time on his hands may turn his attention to someone else's cipher as a work of supererogation. A case in point is that of the cipher known as 'GGG'. This was a relatively simple 'creeping subtractor' system, used by an enemy agent sitting with a telescope at La Linea and reporting what he saw of our shipping or aircraft. This was deciphered as a sideline by Philip Hunt, one of the W/S party, (and later by myself). The only value of its content was that it provided, for a time, a reliable 'crib' into the GGG Enigma machine used by the German spy network, for which reason it was soon handed over to another section of GC & CS.

Yet another 'sidekick' of the cryptographers of German Naval Section was altogether more interesting and not German at all but Italian. In the winter of 1941–42 there was a considerable dearth of W/S traffic, and what there was could be fairly quickly deciphered by the W/S party, which by now had got its eye in. Moreover, the organisation of Naval Section was still somewhat fluid so that manpower could be switched to where it was most needed. At this time the main cipher used by the Italian navy was the Hagelin machine, a Swedish invention commercially and internationally available. It was less problematic than *Schluessel* M but had its own complexities. Every month it was given a new setting which was rapidly broken at Bletchley by three very able young men (one of whom, Colin Thompson, was later to be curator of the Scottish National Gallery). But for a week or so each individual signal had to be deciphered separately by a cryptographic process known as 'rodding'. This was largely and successfully undertaken by the W/S party. The traffic could be interesting, or even of operational importance since it might give the routes chosen for transport and supply shps reinforcing Rommel's army.

But this success, like all good things, came to an end. Regrettably the Americans, although warned against it, decided to use Hagelin for their army traffic. This duly alerted the enemy's cryptographers to Hagelin's vulnerability and led to the Italian navy's going over to something much more difficult. It led also to the reading, by the enemy, of much American traffic, with very tragic results. Perhaps significantly, Hagelin is conspicuous by its absence from the published books.

CREDIT AND CRITICISM OF CRYPTOGRAPHERS

With the manpower available to them the successes attained by the cryptographers might be called reasonably good. What is less clear and more controversial is how well those successes were exploited. Material learnt from hand cipher signals was not only graded as less reliable than Enigma material; it was also given a more restricted circulation. I was once on duty at the Admiralty when a W/S signal about a German ship that was in trouble in the Bight was teleprinted from Bletchley. Both the Admiralty's duty officer and I thought this should be passed to the Air Ministry but it was discovered that the rules forbade it. Again, once on leave I met an old friend who was then in the War Office at the receiving end from Bletchley's Hut 3. His job was to know where and in what strength all units of the German army were at any given moment, especially on the Russian front. He told me he would give a lot to know how much shipping passed east or westbound in the Baltic every day. At that period I was in the habit of deciphering each morning a W/S signal from *Wachtschiff Warnemuende* giving precisely this information. I advised consultation with Naval Section through Hut 3. My friend did this and was told that nothing of the sort was known. Such unreliable information could not be passed to the War Office. Sometimes, too, the identification of U-boats in the Baltic from W/S signals was not sent to the Admiralty until it was confirmed – sometimes days or even weeks later – by the machine.

All this had certain adverse effects on the morale of those working on hand cipher. It brought to a head certain chronic tensions between cryptography and intelligence which were notable at least in Bletchley's Naval Section. It may exemplify the friction between production and sales management that is liable to emerge in any industry. Each party looked somewhat askance at the other. To the intelligence officer cryptographers were apt to appear as unworldly, absent-minded, eccentric, ill-dressed academics. To the cryptographer the intelligence officer could appear to be too political by half and often as a shameless empire builder.

Part of the problem was that cryptography, however successful, does not make a good exhibit for showing to a visiting admiral, who is thought to be happier if he is seeing a map full of flags and pins. Moreover, one intelligence officer could and did complain that a certain cryptographer seemed strangely unmoved when told suddenly that the *Scharnhorst* had been sunk. This might well have been due to his having had no means of knowing that the *Scharnhorst* was at sea and/or to his being at the moment immersed in a long bigram count.

Almost certainly a number of intelligence officers had presupposed that cryptography had its own mystique requiring very special mathematical insights amounting virtually to genius. They were then surprised to find that most cryptographers were in fact fairly ordinary if moderately intelligent people and, further, that a good deal of deciphering owed something to the fortuitous capture of some document such as a code-book or a set of tables, not to mention 'cribs'. In other words, they discovered that there was hardly such a thing as 'pure' cryptography. One holder of high office in Naval Section recorded in an official memorandum that 'in this war we have at last been able to call the bluff of cryptography'. Such an attitude, often made fairly obvious, contributed to the cryptographer's malaise.

If a cryptographer is unsuccessful, for whatever reason, he tends to be forgotten or possibly misjudged. If he is consistently successful his work may be taken for granted or supposed much easier than it actually is. This impression was probably heightened in the minds of the higher powers in Naval Section, who were not without a tinge of male chauvinism, by the fact that some of the Section's best cryptographers were women, not least Ruth Briggs.

A very distinguished cryptographer on the permanent staff of GC & CS was once asked what he regarded as a cryptographer's principal requirements, and replied, 'Oh, I suppose a sharp pencil and piece of squared paper'. There is a grain of truth in this view. Except on the really highest slopes, attained only by a Turing, a Knox, a Welchman or a Max Newman, where quasi-mathematical genius is required, the cryptographer's main requisites are probably patience, accuracy, stamina, a reasonably clear head, some experience and an ability to work with others. This last, teamwork, is important but paradoxically can also be a cause of friction, since it tends to make of the cryptographer a natural democrat who may not fit too easily into a hierarchical system which Naval Section undoubtedly was.

One young lieutenant, RNVR, though able, industrious and a polyglot scholar, was reprimanded for writing an intelligence report which was critical of Admiral Doenitz. He was told that it was most improper for a lieutenant to criticise an admiral in any navy whatsoever.

One set of decisions, taken largely on administrative grounds, contributed not a little to disillusionment in the cryptographic party. This was the deliberate discontinuance of work on three readable German hand ciphers. In each case, admittedly, the intelligence value was diminishing, and in the case of W/S the traffic itself was dwindling, as was its importance as a provider of 'cribs'. Work on the K-code was deemed to have outlived its usefulness once the fighting had moved far inland from the coast, and work on it ceased in August 1944. The decision later in the same month to stop work on the higher grade *Schluessel* Henno was more controversial. With the staff available it was only being partially read; and the staff allegedly was urgently required elsewhere in the Section. Work on W/S was continued till the end of February 1945 and, with its demise, the cryptographic part of German Naval Section was virtually wound up. To some of the cryptographers these measures offended against what to them seemed a first principle, namely, that what was worth an enemy's while to encipher must be worth our while to decipher.

The controversy, particularly over the case of Henno, may have accentuated the cryptographers' occasional grumpiness. What is certain and must certainly be said is that the cryptographers' morale was never for one moment impoverished in the only sense that mattered. Their earlier discontents were mainly over having to do so much besides cryptography, and their final *cri-de-coeur* was a lament at having no more cryptography to do. No one who saw them at work, especially in a period after one of their ciphers had changed, could have doubted their zest and avidity for their own job. It might be said that the cryptographers were sometimes, like the British army, unable to go about their work without swearing. But it will be remembered that the profanity of the British soldiers, though it may have met with frowns from army chaplains, has only once – in the wars against the Maoris – cost them the respect of their opponents. There is no evidence that even Joan of Arc had doubts about the fighting qualities of the 'Goddams'.

Surveillance and Intelligence under the Vichy Regime: The Service du Contrôle Technique, 1939–45

ROGER AUSTIN

Historians of Vichy France have not yet provided an adequate explanation of the ways in which the regime acquired legitimacy, that is to say, how it secured consent from French people. This article is a contribution to that debate by providing an analysis of how the Vichy state developed a surveillance and information gathering network based on a massive interception of private correspondence. The system was vital to Vichy's legitimacy in two ways: first, by sensitive 'listening' to the mood of the public it was able to gauge how best to present those policies which were essential for its very survival and secondly through its pervasive intrusion of individual privacy it helped to create the conditions of fear and mistrust that made concerted opposition to the regime extremely difficult. The organisation and purpose of this system, the *Service du Contrôle Technique* (SCT), has a three-fold importance: first, in revealing the central role played by the military authorities in intelligence gathering within France, it indicates how far some senior officers had gone in redefining the enemy; second, in the way it pursued those individuals whose private communications were regarded as 'suspect', it shows both how insecure the regime was and how essential the SCT was to effective policing; and thirdly, it shows how policy decisions of the highest importance were influenced by the regime's knowledge of public opinion.

The development of the SCT under Vichy can be best understood in three stages: the first, July 1940–March 1941, was an intermediate period during which the organisational structure of military censorship was taken over and its purpose was radically altered; the second, March 1941–May 1942, marks, under Admiral Darlan, a particularly important stage when the SCT activities were a clearly co-ordinated arm of government; and finally between May 1942 and August 1944 Pierre Laval's reorganisation of the SCT to be directly dependent on his own office, represents a period when the SCT was of vital importance to government policies of persuasion and coercion.

JULY 1940 – MARCH 1941

Although the practice of intercepting private correspondence has a long history in France and elsewhere,[1] the organisational structure that Vichy took over and developed was very much the product of the military censorship which had operated during the war of 1914–18 and again from September 1939 to June 1940.

During the Phoney War, letters, phone calls and telegrams were regularly intercepted and systematically exploited by the Fifth Bureau of the *Etat Major de l'Armée*. The operation monitored both civilian and conscript morale and was conducted by military personnel with the co-operation of post office officials.[2] Reports on the mood of the population towards the war, based on a synthesis of the interceptions, were sent monthly from each army region in France to the *Président du Conseil* and to the *Ministère de la Défense Nationale et de la Guerre*.[3] Although a degree of secrecy surrounded the system, certain aspects of its operation were clearly visible: for example, letters which were opened were resealed with a band and stamped with the words 'Opened by the Censor'. In other cases, letters which contained what was regarded as classified information were either stopped or the offending passages were rendered illegible. As we shall see, this was very different from what was to happen under Vichy.

Although wartime censorship was essentially a military operation there were hints during the Phoney War of what was to come later. From the outbreak of war, the Ministry of the Interior began to exert pressure to be allowed greater access to the information that the military authorities were collecting. Although the principle of allowing a representative of the Ministry of the Interior to sit on each local *commission de contrôle* had been conceded by the army in 1924, new instructions in December 1939 gave prefects the right to require local *présidents* of the *contrôle* to hand over copies of their reports.[4] Until July 1940, however, the evidence suggests that the principal function of the *Contrôle Technique* was not internal surveillance as such but rather the monitoring of morale in the war effort.

Within weeks of the defeat and the armistice, however, entirely new perspectives began to open up: although the various postal, telegraphic and telephone *commissions de contrôle* were officially dissolved on 8 July 1940,[5] they continued to operate covertly in the unoccupied zone and in French North Africa. There appear to have been two major reasons for this which corresponded to the twin preoccupations of the army immediately after the defeat. First, the role of the army in maintaining internal order in France is testified to in a variety of letters and statements between June 1940 and July 1941. On 27 June 1940, for example, the *ministre de la guerre* was instructing his generals of the necessity of maintaining order at any price.[6] More emphatically, Huntziger, the new *ministre de la guerre* from 6 September, told them on 25 October that the *mission* (my emphasis) of the army was 'to maintain order'.[7] This reflex was so powerful that it clearly led some senior army officers to redefine the enemy: indeed, the decision to transfer the organisation of the *Contrôle Technique* from the Fifth Bureau to the Second Bureau of the *Etat Major de l'Armée*[8] was not simply an administrative change. The Second Bureau's responsibility was, precisely, that of monitoring 'the enemy' and from 30 July 1940, when they began sending in their first reports based on intercepted correspondence, the first section showed how far the process of redefinition had already gone. It contained a detailed analysis of currents of opposition to the new regime under the heading 'Information of anti-national activities in all their forms'.[9]

While securing internal order remained a military preoccupation throughout the period,[10] it is also quite evident from secret archives that the decision to allow discreet interceptions to continue in July 1940 was to provide 'military and diplomatic information on foreign radio communications'.[11] It was also essential for this operation to escape from what one report from the Second Bureau called 'foreign control'.[12] In this sense, eavesdropping on the occupying authorities salvaged a drop of French military pride and became a means of protecting French national interests in negotiations with Germany. Precisely how much information the Second Bureau obtained on German intentions will remain open to conjecture until French military archives are more fully open to study. What can be safely said at this stage is that the German media were regularly monitored from July 1940[13] and there is some evidence to suggest that the French did succeed in monitoring German communications in France.[14]

One of the ways of concealing the SCT from both the Germans and from the French public was to divest the system of its military surveillance connotations by renaming it the *Service Civil des Contrôles Techniques*. Although the official reason for this was that 'the reduced number of personnel authorised for the Armistice Army have obliged military departments to 'civilianise' several of their essential services',[15] military control of the service was in fact formally recognised when it was attached to the *secrétariat d'état à la guerre* from 1 November 1940.[16] The strength of military control over the operation remained secure until May 1942, not least because the personnel who manned the service were predominantly 'officers on armistice leave'.[17] Although civilians were employed as members of the local *commission de contrôle postal*, they were very much under military authority and required by the army to work away from the department in which they lived.[18]

The function of the surveillance system was thus beginning to take shape: by late autumn 1940, once the decision had been taken to retain the *Contrôle Technique*, the army's experience during the Phoney War and their evident willingness to play a role in maintaining order enabled them to hold on to the operation and redirect its focus to the interior rather than the exterior. At the same time, there is evidence from some local archives that changes in personnel were designed to ensure that controllers were sympathetic to the new regime. Secrecy became of paramount importance within France if the service was to gather reliable information: so it was that in addition to letters being opened as before and resealed with the official band, others were now opened 'discreetly',[19] 'by steam'.[20] The budget to pay for this very extensive operation, 50 million francs by March 1941, was deliberately concealed in the expenses of the *secrétariat à la guerre*.[21]

In this initial period of its existence under Vichy, information gathered by the SCT was primarily used to produce an analysis of 'anti-national activities in any form, the state of opinion, food rationing and production, the state of morale in the French army and all other military matters, economic and financial information, general intelligence on conditions outside France and foreign investigations in France'.[22] Although a parallel function of the system was the search for infringements of the law, it was not yet systematically used in a repressive way to pursue individuals regarded as 'suspect'. Indeed, up to March 1941, prefects were still simply receiving copies of the reports on the mood of the population which each president of the *commission de contrôle* drew up.[23] It was the appearance of Darlan as head of a new administration in which he himself held the key positions of *Vice-Président du Conseil, Affaires étrangères, Intérieur* and *Information* that was to make the *Contrôle Technique* an indispensable part of government machinery.

MARCH 1941 – MAY 1942

Within a month of assuming office in February 1941 Darlan received a detailed report on the operation of the SCT which argued that since it was 'a government arm for investigation and surveillance it would seem logical to attach it to the *Vice-Présidence du Conseil*'.[24] Darlan accepted this view and from 26 March 1941 until May 1942 the SCT operated 'under the supreme authority of the *Vice-Président du Conseil* who gives the *Ministère Secrétaire d'état à la guerre* directives concerning his operation'.[25]

One of the practical implications of this reorganisation was that Darlan gave the SCT a much more sharply defined investigative and repressive function. Very few people were exempt from its operation: high-ranking civil servants such as *inspecteurs de l'Académie* and police inspectors were as likely to have their correspondence intercepted as anybody else. This new purpose, which remained a permanent characteristic of the SCT long after Darlan had disappeared from power, was outlined to all prefects in the unoccupied zone of France on 22 March 1941:

> The role of these interceptions can be put in two categories: one related to information gathering, the other concerned with possible infringements, crimes and offences.
>
> It seems to me that the results obtained in the second category are still inadequate.[26]

Further clarification on how prefects were to exploit the information revealed in intercepted letters, phone calls and telegrams was sent in April, May and June.[27] By July 1941 the number of affairs revealed by the SCT and under investigation in the unoccupied zone had doubled from 1,346 to 2,866: each month officials in the SCT sent the prefect 'a monthly report of interceptions likely to lead to police, judicial or administrative investigation'.[28] The prefects took appropriate action and sent the Minister of the Interior a detailed monthly report on how each case had come to light, what form of investigation was being carried out and what results had been achieved. The reports also contained a request to place under particularly close surveillance those individuals whose correspondence the prefect believed to be suspect.[29] These monthly reports, which continued until at least November 1943,[30] provide a remarkable picture of the political, economic and criminal offences that were revealed in intercepted correspondence. From September 1941 to April 1942, it is possible to see both the total number of those under surveillance, the extent of differences between geographical departments and the sort of suspected offences that were investigated.[31] Between September 1941 and February 1942 the list of those whose correspondence was systematically intercepted in Vichy's unoccupied zone increased from 1,086 to 1,340. Whereas in the Corrèze and the Aude there was nobody, according to the prefects, whose correspondence required particular surveillance, in the Hérault there were 39, all but one of whom were listed for political affairs rather than economic or ciminal ones. While these differences are explicable in terms of varying densities of population, and varying degrees of zeal employed by SCT officials, prefects and investigating bodies like the *Police Judiciaire*, certain common traits are discernible across the unoccupied zone. Although it was possible for individuals to be investigated for nothing more than what one report called 'suspect conversation' or being a 'possible listener to Gaullist Radio',[32] the available evidence does not suggest an overwhelming preoccupation with enforcing political conformity. Roughly one half of a sample of the investigations were for suspected economic or financial offences such as black market affairs, illegal transportation of goods etc., one third could be classified as political and the remainder were criminal affairs.[33] This preoccupation with what might be called economic dissent may lead historians to re-assess the relative importance of this form of oppositional behaviour compared with the well researched field of political resistance.

As a means of uncovering political, economic or criminal deviancy, the system had a number of in-built weaknesses: first, although over 2 million letters were intercepted every month in Vichy France up to May 1942[34] and an even larger number thereafter,[35] this represented less than 10 per cent of the total correspondence in Vichy France.[36] With the exception of incoming post to listed suspects, all other interceptions were made on a random basis. The same was true for telephone calls and telegrams. Clearly, therefore, the SCT could only pick up a small percentage of the total volume of potentially suspect correspondence. The second weakness of the system was that since its value depended upon secrecy, incriminating evidence from intercepted letters or phone calls could not be used to trap suspects into a confession. As the *procureur général* in Montpellier wrote to the *Garde des Sceaux* in 1942:

> I wish to underline how difficult it is to proceed with an enquiry based on interceptions. Enquiries are invariably hindered by investigators being unable to produce the damning evidence which would lead to a confession.[37]

However reluctant the judiciary were to expose the system, knowledge of the SCT was known to obvious opponents of the regime like the communists as early as mid 1941 and to a certain number of teachers, schoolchildren and educational officials by May 1942.[38] A natural caution about what could be safely said by precisely those sections of society most likely to oppose the regime was a further weakness in the system and goes some way to explaining why only a very small percentage of the total volume of correspondence intercepted appears to have led to successful convictions.[39]

The value of the SCT to Vichy as a means of detecting either opposition or criminality cannot be judged solely in terms of the level of convictions. It is almost certain that the secret activities of the SCT and the subsequent investigations by the police encouraged individuals to believe they were being spied on and denounced by neighbours, workmates or those around them. Since they had no means of knowing that intercepted private letters or phone calls were the source of information which led to them being investigated, it was natural to suppose that they were the victims of denunciation. This atmosphere of suspicion and fear, so terrifyingly evoked in *Le Corbeau*,[40] undoubtedly fuelled further denunciations. Although Vichy was forced to legislate to put a stop to anonymous denunciations,[41] it was the regime itself which had encouraged the process with its appeal to root out internal enemies and its surreptitious violation of individual privacy. The decision to stop further denunciations was not a sign of 'weakness' by Vichy but a blunt recognition that the state apparatus could not cope with the flood of often misleading and venomous accusations.

It may be claimed that the value of the SCT as an instrument of surveillance to Vichy was that it succeeded in making the population cautious and mistrustful of each other, and this was vital in weakening the bonds of trust that concerted opposition to the regime relied upon.

In addition to the role of the SCT outlined so far, Darlan made it clear to prefects that its other function was to monitor public opinion. Indeed, from August 1941 to May 1942 structured questions were sent each week from the *Service Central du Contrôle Technique* to each departmental *commission de contrôle* to act as a framework for an analysis of the mood of the population.[42] Although the questions changed from one month to another, they were designed to find out whether, in general, the public approved of Pétain, Darlan, and collaboration with Germany and whether they thought Germany would win the war. In addition to these broad questions there were more specific ones: for example, in early September 1941, SCT agents were asked to find out 'Is there support for armed intervention by the United States?', 'Is the Marshal's message of 12 August approved?', 'Are the measures taken against Freemasonry supported?'. Later, in January 1942 new questions revealed evolution in the war situation: 'Is the entry of the USA and Japan into the war favourable to French interests?', 'Are Russian successes creating a new fear of communism?'. Others were directed to finding out how popular domestic policy was through questions on the Legion, rationing, prisoners of war and the work charter.[43] Replies to these questions were based on an analysis of about 350,000 letters each week for the whole of the southern zone of Vichy France.

The nature of the questions asked, particularly compared with the way in which Laval used the SCT to monitor public opinion from May 1942, suggests that Darlan wanted to keep in touch with the public to ensure that his policies had popular support, to monitor deteriorating internal security and also to guide him in the new deal he was exploring with Germany. We know that, at about this time, Darlan received a report from the Combined Forces' Second Bureau which argued very strongly that they should be playing a much greater role in advising the regime through providing high-quality intelligence and that France's best interests would be served by a policy of collaboration with Germany. As their report concluded,

> Collaboration, necessary in the event of a short war, becomes an absolute necessity from which it is impossible to escape, if the war drags on.[44]

If such a policy were to be implemented Darlan knew that he would have to carry public opinion with him: it is entirely consistent with what we know about Darlan's personality and approach to government that he should wish to be fully informed about whether this policy would be approved of by the public. Indeed it is quite possible that Darlan's uncertainty on how far he could proceed with a Franco-German military partnership was caused by a recognition that the public were alternately hostile or reticent on this issue. Darlan's opportunism was seen as vacillation, at least by Laval who commented, 'Darlan used to read the communiqués every morning in order to decide whether to be for or against Germany that day'.[45]

Darlan's need for popular acclaim and his keen sense of policy as the art of the possible made it imperative for him to ensure that at home and abroad he was sailing in a direction approved by the majority of the public. His need for reassurance on this meant that the information provided by the SCT was essential: however, rather than question the reliability of the views expressed, Darlan believed that the accuracy of the opinions depended solely on keeping the SCT's operation highly secret.

A flood of warnings in October 1941 that copies of intercepted correspondence had been too widely disseminated culminated in the following note from Darlan to ministers:

> These repeated revelations are not only contrary to explicit instructions but risk damaging a precious source of information and intelligence on all matters which, in reply to my letter on 6 September 1941, you indicated were both useful and valuable. It has been demonstrated that the least publicity on the interceptions temporarily paralyses the expression of public opinion and thus denies the government of useful intelligence.[46]

Darlan's use of the SCT operation to monitor public opinion provided him with information which was not only useful to his calculations in foreign policy but helped to fine-tune his action within France. Analysis of intercepted comments on food shortages and the black market enabled Darlan to see that a selective policy of attacking 'professional dealers' rather than harassing individuals whose hunger had pushed them into making illegal purchases, would be understood and appreciated by the public at large.[47]

But whereas Darlan appeared to listen to the hopes and fears of the French people and then take action accordingly, Laval's approach on his return to power in April 1942 was markedly different.

MAY 1942 – AUGUST 1944

When Laval was comparing his attitude with that of Darlan who read communiqués before making up his mind what policy to adopt, he said: 'I am not interested in communiqués; I am pursuing a policy from which nothing will make me alter course'.[48] Supporting evidence for the accuracy of this observation can be found in the way that Laval used the SCT: by May 1942 the set of detailed questions to monitor public opinion was discontinued,[49] and the following month Laval began the process of totally reshaping the structure and the purpose of the system. In August 1942 a detailed secret report to all ministers[50] revealed that the SCT was now under the direct authority of *le Chef du Gouvernement*.[51] Military personnel were progressively squeezed out of its direction and its local operations.

The only satisfactory way of explaining this exclusion of the military authorities from the SCT was Laval's desire to concentrate under his direct control all the most sensitive instruments of government. He held the offices of *chef du gouvernement, ministre de l'Intérieur, des Affaires Etrangères et de l'Information*; it was an essential corollary of co-ordinating government policy in these fields that Laval should control all branches of the state's surveillance and information network. It was not that Laval was particularly concerned about his personal popularity: as he said in June 1942, 'I have always liked my country too much to worry about being popular: I have to fulfil my role as leader'.[52] It was rather that having decided on a policy of collaboration with Germany he now wished to use the information from the SCT to exercise the maximum persuasion and most effective coercion on the public.

Henceforth, nobody could be exempted from surveillance except by personal authority of Laval: each *inspecteur régional* was to keep a file (*fiches*) based on interceptions, information from which could be passed on to 'authorities empowered to ask for surveillance'. It was this system which immeasurably strengthened Vichy's policing of the country and in particular enabled it to track down Jews and opponents of the regime.[53] Alongside this function, discreetly described as helping in the discovery of 'infringements of laws and regulations', Laval wished to *mould* public opinion both by seizing any communications which contradicted government policy and by using knowledge of private attitudes to shape government tactics. These concerns led Laval to take a growing interest in how best to present the regime's policies to the public and particularly the best strategy for handling those decisions most likely to generate opposition to the regime.

Policy towards the Jews was a case in point: at a meeting of the *Conseil des Ministres* in late June 1942, the issue of how to find a solution to German pressure which would also be acceptable to the French public was very much in evidence:

> The Head of Government then turned to an extremely delicate issue: the Jewish question. As we know this had been resolved in Germany in an extremely severe way. French opinion would find it hard to accept that similar measures be taken in France.[54]

A week later, having already decided to use a census to discriminate between French Jews and foreign ones, Laval indicated that 'special measures might be envisaged for those Jews who have arrived in France since September 1939'. The minutes of the meeting added that Pétain believed that this distinction 'is fair and will be understood by the public'.[55] In fact, as reports from the SCT showed in August, Pétain was only partly right: although reports from one major city in the south noted that the round-up of foreign Jews had taken place 'with the complicity and help of the population',[56] SCT agents in Cannes, Nice and Béziers reported 'the indignation of quite a large number of correspondents'.[57] This miscalculation by the regime on what public response was likely to be on the Jewish question led to changes and an increasingly sophisticated use of the SCT.

In spite of the German occupation of the southern zone in November 1942 Vichy not only managed at first to conceal SCT from the occupying authorities but, from 15 January 1943, began to improve the ways in which SCT information could be used. Although the points of interception remained in what had been the southern zone, the far greater volume of communications now possible between northern and southern France enabled SCT officials to analyse the mood of the population throughout the country. Moreover, from early 1943, Laval received a bi-monthly report based on interceptions which made specific suggestions about how the government should present its case: the first reports, for example, argued that:

> Public opinion never takes into account the *negative results* obtained by the Government particularly in its negotiations with the occupying forces. This method of 'governmental exposés' on the radio would reduce this ingratitude, raise the prestige of the Government and rally to it many of its supporters.[58]

In March it was claimed that 'Philippe Henriot is sometimes cited as possessing the range of qualities needed by such an "air wave supremo' '.[59] From this point onwards, it becomes clear that the increased prominence given to Henriot and the themes of his radio broadcasts were influenced in a very direct way by the known preoccupations of the public as revealed in intercepted correspondence.[60] Indeed, so well did the system work that when the Germans finally discovered the scale of the SCT operation and ordered it to be stopped, Laval was able to persuade them that at least part of it should stay in French hands.

The arguments he used were extremely revealing of the general aim of preserving French 'sovereignty' and of the way in which, by late 1943, Laval saw the purpose of SCT: in the face of von Runstedt's demand that only the postal interceptions be carried out by the French,[61] Laval told Pétain:

> In particular, on questions of food supply and police, the interception of telephone calls and telegrams often enables me to act very effectively. These interceptions also allow me to know at any moment the state of opinion and take necessary measures accordingly.[62]

Later, in February 1944, in a note to the *Délégation Française auprès de la Commission Allemande d'Armistice* at Wiesbaden, Laval tried to convince the Germans that the effectiveness of French policing depended on maintaining the totality of the SCT in French hands:

> At the very moment when, in agreement with the competent German Authorities, all police powers have been placed in the hands of M. Joseph Darnand, *Secrétaire Général au Maintien de l'Ordre*, to help him cope with a difficult situation, it is in neither French nor German interests to reduce the sources of information available to the Government in such a marked way.[63]

Further evidence that policing and internal security had become Laval's major pre-occupation can be found in both the decision to exclude prefects from receiving SCT reports and in the increasingly sophisticated analysis of public attitudes to the maquis and the Resistance.

By February 1944, with responsibility for law enforcement now concentrated in Darnard's hands, it was decided that prefects could no longer be trusted with the sensitive information that the SCT was still providing from intercepted mail.[64] Although Laval had had to concede to the Germans their right to intercept phone calls and telegrams in February 1944, communication by letter continued to provide the SCT with vital information on private attitudes to food supply, to the Allies, Henriot's broadcasts, the Milice and the Resistance right up to August 1944. What is particularly interesting about Vichy's analysis of public opinion in 1944 is that it reveals the importance attributed to issues like the Resistance by the public, it provides textual citations of attitudes attributed to the social class of the correspondent and finally, its conclusions can be compared with a parallel operation carried out by the Gaullists based in Algeria.

For example, in June 1944, the *inspection régionale* in Montpellier indicated that the subject most frequently referred to was 'food supply and rationing' followed by 'bombing raids', 'the landing' with what it called 'terrorism' rated sixth. Its analysis of attitudes to 'terrorism' showed that, although there was an overwhelming feeling of 'disapproval and fear' rather than 'approval' (3,706 references to 396), the strength of this disapproval had weakened slightly between May and June (Disapproval: 4,833 references to 3,706; Approval: 25 : 396).[65] In July, the SCT analysis for the whole of France found that twice as many correspondents were hostile to the maquis as those in favour (13,245 : 7,131) and that disapproval of 'terrorism' was indicated by 22,920 writers against 1,804.[66] It would clearly be unwise to regard this on its own as an accurate measure of the views of all sections of public opinion: given what we have already said about people's knowledge of the system, it is reasonable to suppose that many opponents of Vichy were unwilling to express their views in letters.

However, a certain amount of corroborative evidence for these attitudes can be found in communications intercepted by the Gaullist authorities. They had set up their own *Service du Contrôle Technique* in January 1943 initially under the authority of the *Haut Commissariat en Afrique Française* and from February 1943 under the *commandement en chef français civil et militaire*.[67] By September 1943 they were intercepting 500,000 letters a month in North Africa and by February 1944, when the Service was directed by the *Comité Français de Libération Nationale*, its analysis extended to metropolitan France. The CFLN was well aware of Vichy's SCT and found that its reports contained what one of their agents called 'useful indications on the state of opinion'.[68] Partly for this reason and also to avoid drawing attention to their own interceptions, the CFLN does not appear to have exposed Vichy's system.

What their own reports show is that from January to August 1944, after initial sympathy for de Gaulle, the population were increasingly worried about what was referred to as 'frightening banditry' (13–20 May); 'Alongside the "maquis", a false maquis has appeared' (20–27 May); 'next to genuine resistance fighters, trouble makers have showed up who are committing crimes, thefts and violations of the law (27 May–3 June).[69] Reports like these no doubt really do reflect the natural anxieties of the French public in the last months of the Vichy regime. But reports can also be seen as containing unconscious projections of the authority which commissioned them: in this case, they reflect a curious bond between the two parallel SCTs; both, because of their military associations, were anxious to avoid civil disorder, and may therefore have 'looked for' evidence in intercepted communications which confirmed their own fears. It is also clear that the communists succeeded in bypassing both systems and were regarded with equal suspicion in both Vichy and Algiers. The September 1943 report in Gaullist North Africa, for example, contained a sharp prediction of things to come in its analysis of the political activity of the communist party:

> In relation to the indigenous population, the party is pursuing a pro-Arab policy in which the Arabs are seen as 'a mass element': this policy is giving rise to considerable apprehension on the situation of the French in post-war North Africa.[70]

Observations like these help to explain why it was that when the SCT operations were finally closed down in mainland France in December 1944, they continued to operate in North Africa.[71] By a curious twist of history, the Gaullist 'liberators' of mainland France were soon to be perceived as the 'occupying authorities' of North Africa, at least by part of the population.

Conclusions about the function and importance of the SCT in our understanding of the Vichy period represent two sides of the same coin. On one side, Vichy's effective policing of France relied to a very great extent on the investigative and repressive side of the SCT which Darlan introduced and Laval developed. In future it will be difficult to talk about the role of the police in Vichy France without reference to the SCT. On the other side of the coin, it is clear that historians have underestimated the extent to which the regime felt the need to keep in touch with public opinion, either to be guided by it or to manipulate it. In part, this was a sign of insecurity but also, especially from 1942, an illustration of Laval's determination to use every available instrument to coerce or persuade the public to follow the course he had set out upon. In spite of the obvious weaknesses of relying completely on SCT reports, there is no doubt that Vichy derived considerable moral comfort from their conclusions, particularly in 1943–44 when they indicated widescale approval of Henriot's broadcasts, and 'indignation, sometimes violent' at the news of his assassination.[72] This evidence, taken with public reaction to the maquis, enabled Vichy to believe that it still had support. In this sense, therefore, the SCT became increasingly vital to the regime's capacity to believe it had some sort of popular mandate to continue governing the country. This not only helps to explain why Laval held on to power as long as he did but also provides some explanation of how the Vichy regime retained legitimacy in many areas of the country right up to the moment of the transition of power to the Allies and de Gaulle.

NOTES

I would like to thank the University of Ulster, the British Academy and the 27 Foundation Award for supporting this research in 1984 and to the French Embassy in London which enabled me to corroborate my initial findings. I would also like to express my gratitude to Roderick Kedward for his comments on a draft of this paper.

1. Jean Tulard, 'Les Français sous surveillance', *L'Histoire*, No. 32, March 1981.
2. Archives of the Service Historique de l'Armée de Terre, Vincennes. Conseil Supérieur de la Défense Nationale 2N 263. Contrôle PTT 23 September 1939, 'Organisation du Service Postal', 21 September 1939.
3. Archives Nationales (hereafter AN) F 7 14924 and AJ^{41} 25.
4. Archives Départementales de la Lozère (hereafter ADL) VI^{M2} 19. Instructions from Minister of the Interior to prefects, 12 December 1939.
5. Conseil Supérieur de la Défense Nationale 7N 2462, Note from le Général d'Armée, Ministre de la Guerre, to Generals commanding Regions 7, 9, 12 to 18, Clermont-Ferrand, 6 July 1940.
6. Archives de l'Armée de Terre. 7N 2462.
7. AN AJ^{41} 62. Note to Senior Army Officers 25 October 1940.
8. Archives Départementales de l'Ardèche (hereafter ADA), CAB 517, Note from M. le Général Cdt de la XVe Div. Militaire, 24 September 1940.
9. AN AJ^{41} 25. See report No. 6 for 6–12 September 1940.
10. See for example their concern for order in the Chantiers de la Jeunesse, Roger Austin, 'The Chantiers de la Jeunesse in Languedoc 1940–1944', *French Historical Studies*, Spring, 1983.
11. AN AJ^{41} 725.
12. AN AJ^{41} 725. Note on 3 August 1940.
13. AN AJ^{41} 62.
14. AN AJ^{41} 722.
15. AN F 60 514. Note on 18 March 1941.
16. AN BB30 1723. Note on 1 November 1940.
17. AN F 60 514. Note on 18 November 1941.
18. AN F 60 569. Note on 5 September 1941.
19. AN F 90 12101. Report on 19 September 1940. AN BB30 1723.
20. ADA CAB 517. ADL VI^{M2} 19. Note on 2 October 1940.
21. AN F 60 514. Report on 18 March 1941.
22. AN F 7 14927. Report on 12 September 1940.
23. ADA CAB 517. Note from Minister of Interior to prefects on 13 October 1940.
24. AN F 60 514. Note on 18 March 1941.
25. AN BB30 1723. Decree No. 1393 of 26 March 1941.
26. Archives Départementales du Gard (hereafter ADG) CAB 649. Ministère de l'Intérieur aux prefets, Cab. Pol. No. 136, 22 March 1941.
27. ADG CAB 649. Circular of 22 April 1941. AN F 60 514. Circulars on 12 May 1941 and 14 June 1941.
28. ADL VI^{M2} 19 July 1941.
29. AN F 60 514.
30. ADA CAB 517.
31. AN F 60 514. I have also been able to draw upon John Dixon's research in the Archives Départementales de la Haute Vienne at Limoges on this point.
32. AN F 60 514. Reports from Vaucluse and Var, 26 April 1942.
33. AN F 60 514. ADA CAB 517.
34. AN F 7 14926.
35. AN F 7 14929. For the month of January 1944 the number of interceptions was 2,236,120 letters, 1,573,763 telegrams and 92,000 recorded phone calls.
36. This figure is based on the assumption that the percentage of communications intercepted in the Ardèche was typical of the rest of France. ADA CAB 517.
37. AN BB30 1723. Letter 2 December 1942.
38. Roger Austin, 'Political Surveillance and Ideological Control: Teachers in the Midi,

1940–1944' in R. Kedward and R. Austin (eds.), *Vichy France and the Resistance: Ideology and Culture* (London: Croom Helm, 1985).
39. AN F 60 514. Report on 20 August 1941. In this month only four per cent of the intercepted correspondence in Vichy France led to successful prosecution. This is the only month so far for which I have been able to discover reliable figures.
40. *Le Corbeau*, directed by G. H. Clouzot, 1943. For script see *L'Avant-scène du Cinéma*, No. 186, April 1977.
41. ADA CAB 668. Note on 2 January 1942. This was followed by a law on 8 October 1943 threatening imprisonment and a fine to those found guilty of denunciation.
42. AN F 7 14926. Note de Service CT 117, 20 August 1941.
43. AN F 7 14926.
44. AN F 60 514. Note sur le rôle consultatif des 2° Bureaux, s.d. but early 1941.
45. Quoted by R. Aron, *Histoire de Vichy* (Paris: Fayard, 1954), Vol. II, pp. 182–3.
46. AN BB30 1723. Although this note is dated 9 October 1942, this must be a misprint for 1941.
47. AN F 1A 3671. L'Amiral de la Flotte to Ministers and Regional prefects 16 February 1942, Cabinet No. 913/SG.
48. AN F 7 14927.
50. AN BB30 1723. L'Instruction d'Application du Décret Secret No. 2384 du 1 Août 1942.
51. Laval delegated responsibility for the running of the SCT to an Inspecteur Général, whose appointment was confirmed on 23 August 1942. AN BB30 1723.
52. Quoted by Aron, op. cit., p. 182.
53. Jacques Poujol, 'Les "Mouchards" de la France Occupée', *L'Histoire*, No. 5, November 1982.
54. Réunion du Conseil des Ministres, 26 June 1942, Archives of the Institut d'Histoire du Temps Présent (IHTP).
55. Réunion du Conseil des Ministres, 3 July 1942, Archives of IHTP.
56. AN F 7 14930. Report to the Commission Centrale de Contrôle Téléphonique, August 1942.
57. Ibid.
58. AN F 7 14934. Suggestions inspirées par l'étude du Contrôle des Correspondances Postales, Téléphoniques et Télégraphiques pendant le mois de décembre 1942.
59. AN F 7 14934. Report dated 10 March 1943.
60. AN F 41 290.
61. AN AJ[41] 1106. Note from Commandant en Chef 'Ouest' au gouvernement français, 18 October 1943.
62. AN AJ[41] 722. Laval to Pétain, 25 October 1943.
63. AN AJ[41] 722. Note on 16 February 1944.
64. The decision to exclude prefects can be found in ADL VI[M2] 19. Note from Inspecteur Général to Inspecteur Régional, February 1944.
65. AN F 7 14932.
66. AN F 7 14929.
67. AN F 7 14935.
68. AN F 1A 3744. Gaullist analysis of value of Vichy's SCT report in Toulon, January 1944.
69. AN F 7 14935.
70. AN F 1A 3806. Synthèse 13–19 September 1943.
71. ADL VI[M2] 19.
72. AN F 7 14933.

For Product Safety Concerns and Information please contact our EU
representative GPSR@taylorandfrancis.com
Taylor & Francis Verlag GmbH, Kaufingerstraße 24, 80331 München, Germany

www.ingramcontent.com/pod-product-compliance
Lightning Source LLC
Chambersburg PA
CBHW070623300426
44113CB00010B/1635